T0326360

The Patriot

German Film Classics

Series Editors
Gerd Gemünden, Dartmouth College
Johannes von Moltke, University of Michigan

Advising Editors
Anton Kaes, University of California-Berkeley
Eric Rentschler, Harvard University

Editorial Board

Also in the series:

Fitzcarraldo, by Lutz Koepnick
The Golem, How He Came into the World, by Maya Barzilai
Phoenix, by Brad Prager
Toni Erdmann, by Gerd Gemünden
Warning Shadows, by Anjeana K. Hans
The White Ribbon, by Fatima Naqvi
Wings of Desire, by Christian Rogowski

THE PATRIOT
RICHARD LANGSTON

 CAMDEN HOUSE

First published 2021 by Camden House

Camden House is an imprint of Boydell & Brewer Inc.
668 Mt. Hope Avenue, Rochester, NY 14620, USA
and of Boydell & Brewer Limited
PO Box 9, Woodbridge, Suffolk IP12 3DF, UK
www.boydellandbrewer.com

Cover image: From movie poster for *The Patriot*, used by courtesy of Alexander Kluge, all rights reserved

ISBN-13: 978-1-64014-076-9

Library of Congress Cataloging-in-Publication Data

CIP data is available from the Library of Congress.

This publication is printed on acid-free paper.
Printed in the United States of America.

Publication of this book was supported by a grant from the German Film Institute (GFI) of the University of Michigan Department of Germanic Languages & Literatures.

CONTENTS

ACKNOWLEDGMENTS

Alexander Kluge's prize-winning feature film debut *Yesterday Girl* (1966) may count for many as the classic Kluge *film* but it is his substantial work as not just filmmaker but also author and theoretician that influenced my decision to contribute a volume on *The Patriot* (1979) to the Camden House German Film Classics series. *The Patriot* is cinema, prose, and Frankfurt School theory all wrapped up in one. *The Patriot* is, in other words, classic *Kluge*. In the summer of 2019, I asked Kluge at the Centre culturel international de Cerisy-la-Salle why this film is one for the ages. What would his film's heroine and her unusual patriotism look like in the new millennium? "We need to search for new loyalties in the twenty-first century," he replied without hesitation. This is why he began breathing new life into his heroine just a few short years ago. Constantly changing over time, patriotism of the particular (*das Besondere*) is shaped by an antipathy to any and all forms of centralized power and remains one of, if not *the* cornerstone of Kluge's aesthetic. It can be found in his first stories and films from the sixties and continues to inform his writing and museum installations in 2021. It therefore goes without saying that the following essay would not have been possible without all the many dialogues I've had with Kluge over the years. No amount of gratitude can repay him for his generosity. Thanks also goes to Gülsen Döhr, Beata Wiggen, and, above all, Barbara Barnak, who provided me access to Kluge's second collaboration with Khvan de la Cruz, *Orphea*, before it debuted at the 2020 Berlinale. Without Johannes von Moltke's support, this essay would simply not have seen the light of day. I am also extremely indebted to Gerd Gemünden, Jim Walker, and the manuscript's anonymous reviewer for providing me with invaluable feedback. Their intellectual labor made this book a collaboration in the truest sense.

The Patriot

What's in a Title?

World cinema has no shortage of films about patriots, and German film history is certainly no exception. In fact, one subset of films within this genre unabashedly announces its subject matter with its very titles. Consider, for example, émigré Ernst Lubitsch's 1928 Hollywood biopic *The Patriot* about Count Pahlen's plan to conspire against mad Czar Paul I of Russia, or Karl Ritter's 1937 Nazi propaganda film *The Patriots* about a German World War I pilot shot down behind enemy lines. There is also Rudi Kurz's 1971 film *Artur Becker: Portrait of a Young Patriot*, broadcast on East German television, which recounts the life of the revered antifascist resistance fighter who fell in the Spanish Civil War. And then there's Roland Emmerich's 2000 blockbuster *The Patriot*, a fanciful vehicle for Mel Gibson who plays a militiaman in the American Revolutionary War. If patriots are political subjects whose dearly held ideals of their imagined community run so deep that they take up arms to change the course of history, then patriot films quite often advance heroes designed to embody that desired history. If judged by its title alone, Alexander Kluge's 1979 feature *The Patriot* will surely appear to newcomers like another installment in this revisionist tradition. Cinephiles familiar with Kluge's film and its considerable reception will certainly know, however, how far-removed Kluge's work is from any such affirmative patriotism. One early critic argued, for example, that Kluge's film puts forward a "counter-history" critical of the histories found in German books, schools, and libraries.[1] In light of debates on the burdens of being German raging in the seventies, another critic went farther, arguing that the film's nomadic trek through the German past, present, and imagined futures reflects an emergent "new patriotism," one that interrogated "origin and identity" in search of alternative historiographies.[2] Still another framed this new patriotism as nothing other than a special form of German mourning: "By making history bleed, Kluge wants to bring the past back to life, but neither as spectacle nor even as documentary simulacrum."[3] If patriot films traditionally seek to reconstruct the past into a propitious history, then Kluge's willfully sought to deconstruct any and all such histories.

In spite of its exceptional status among not just German but arguably all patriot films, screening Kluge's *The Patriot* over forty years after its debut poses considerable opportunities and challenges alike, and not just for its English-language viewers. For one, Kluge's story of Gabi Teichert, a late-1970s high school history teacher troubled by the lingering reverberations of Germany's disastrous past, couldn't be timelier in light of the recent rise in nativism, patriotism, and domestic terrorism on both sides of the Atlantic.[4] Rather than abandoning patriotism to those inclined to wield violence in hopes of changing the course of their country's history, Kluge's intervention shows twenty-first-century audiences just how futile patriotism's recourse to violence is. To change history presupposes that we know what it is made of, and what Gabi reveals is not just how elusive that knowledge is but also an alternative relationship to the past and the future, one mediated by film, that is no less patriotic but far more productive. Complicating matters further is, however, the nature of Kluge's material. From a twenty-first-century perspective, the German history in *The Patriot* invariably appears like a strange message in a bottle from a far-off past place and time wholly unrelated to current affairs in Germany, the European Union, or the increasingly distant English-speaking world. At face value, reunified Germany under the leadership of Chancellor Angela Merkel is worlds apart from tumultuous Cold War West Germany under the leadership of Chancellor Helmut Schmidt. Shot between November 1977 and 1979, when the wounds from

West Germany's worst scourge of domestic terrorism were still fresh, *The Patriot* incorporates only the most oblique of references to the chaos unfolding around it.[5] Digging up the abundance of artifacts from German history featured in *The Patriot* and then explicating its relevance for bygone German social history runs the risk of underscoring just how antiquated and alien its qualities are when compared to our very different present-day perspective.

How then might we approach Kluge's *The Patriot* with an eye to the present? What makes *The Patriot* a film for the ages? How can we better understand Gabi's history lessons in situ *and* unlock their relevance for future times and places? As to whether such an endeavor is even feasible at all, Kluge has made clear that reimagining Gabi Teichert's story for the twenty-first century is indeed a challenge. In his 2015 short *Where Have All the Flowers Gone?* he re-casts actress Hannelore Hoger to play the very same excavator of history she played as Gabi in *The Patriot* almost forty years earlier. In fact, the 2015 short clearly announces its intention of remaking the 1979 film by reenacting Hoger's very same entrance in *The Patriot* when she stands before a mirror and puts on her lipstick (figs. 1 and 2). After "making herself up," Hoger ventures outside with her shovel, but instead of unearthing German history as she did in *The Patriot*—where the evil flowers of German history once grew, she now finds stones in tidy stacks—she happens upon a broken window through

Figures 1 and 2. *From left to right*: "Gabi Teichert makes herself up. Next to the mirror is a shovel. She grabs it and throws it over her shoulder." Alexander Kluge, dir., *The Patriot*, 1979. © Kairos Film. "Hannelore Hoger as excavator on the move." Alexander Kluge, dir., "'Where Have All the Flowers Gone?'" 2015. © Kairos Film.

which she spies scenes from the G7 summit held in the Bavarian Alps that same year and the Islamic State's contemporaneous campaigns of terror and destruction. An entirely different history far removed from her own unfolds before her eyes. As its title suggests, Kluge's 2015 reanimation of Gabi Teichert poses a question: What will Gabi hitch her patriotic loyalties to in a globalized world in which German history appears inert? It is, however, not enough just to ask what the new object of Gabi's patriotism might be in the twenty-first century, for that presumes we understand why Gabi is patriotic in the first place. Is it a personal dissatisfaction with having to teach the disasters of German history to her students? Is it her profession's precarious position in the late seventies when the Federal Republic of Germany ousted public schoolteachers who harbored left-wing sympathies? Or is it perhaps simply her gender? The German title of Kluge's film is, after all, *Die Patriotin*, the accurate translation of which would be *The Female Patriot*, not *The Patriot*, as it has been most frequently called in English.

The following reconsideration of Kluge's 1979 masterpiece contends that we can only recognize the contemporary relevance of Gabi's story when we discern the other side of history. To do so, we must recognize that alongside his shorts and features, Kluge, together with the philosopher Oskar Negt, also donned the mantle of social theorist. It is in their gigantic second collaboration, *History and Obstinacy*, commenced in the fall of 1978, where history's opposite—labor power—finds its most robust formulation.[6] Written while Kluge shot *The Patriot*, *History and Obstinacy* defines work as that "human ability to change matter purposefully." "Labor," he goes on, "not only consists of commodity production, but also engenders social relations and develops community."[7] In other words, homelands are made of hard work that assumes Herculean proportions. If patriotism is indeed another word for the desire to change history purposefully, and history, in turn, is understood materialistically as a function of the labor conditions that capitalism determines, then a twofold crisis of labor lies at the heart of both Kluge's film and its contemporary relevance. First of all, why must the historical organization of labor always result in catastrophe? Secondly, if resistance is a form of labor, too, then what sorts of labor can intervene in this juggernaut and therewith constitute alternative communities opposed to this destruction? In his seminal essay on the film, Anton Kaes characterized Kluge's approach to history as "nomadic and analytic" as well as "sensual and unmethodical."[8] In order to screen Kluge's film anew, we must not dismiss this scholarly emphasis on German history altogether in favor of an entirely new optic focused on labor. On the contrary, what the present book's sequential account of Gabi's ten attempts at forging a more patriotic history brings into focus is the nature of her resistance to the narratives found in history books: her obstinate work seeks out increasingly arcane forms of what Kluge and Negt call "intelligence labor." Unlike manual or industrial laborers, those capable of producing critical intelligence—e.g., "teachers, journalists, clergymen"— are uniquely suited for constituting or, in this case, transforming the public sphere and history, too.[9] As will be established in the following pages, the thrust of Gabi's intelligence labor is both critical and utopian. What's more, her obstinacy is caught within what Theodor W. Adorno, one of Kluge's mentors, once called "the wrong state of things" that perpetually preempts utopia's realization.[10] That a female character is the one who performs this mental labor requires further consideration as well, for the simple reason that older forms of the public sphere long excluded female experience. Kluge's attention to gender difference, as we shall see shortly, is not without its problems. Nevertheless, identity and difference remain essential concerns, especially as we turn in our closing reflections to the question of labor and the diminishing possibilities for resistance in the globalized twenty-first century. In the 2020 film *Orphea*, one of Kluge's very recent returns to the feature film after a long hiatus, the outsider status of the Gabi-like figure Orphea assumes new mythical proportions and her obstinacy goes to new extremes in an effort to undo the fates of globalization. This new story, like Gabi's, ends in failure. Even so, what remains constant over time for Kluge's filmmaking is its tenacious attempt to transcend the shortcomings of direct action. Kluge's films both old and new insist on operating as a construction site where the conditions for critical intelligence can emerge within the minds of its spectators.

Alexander Kluge and the Trouble with the Female Patriot

For newcomers to Kluge's *The Patriot*, it's certainly helpful, first, to know a bit about this singular (West) German director. Considered one of the founding architects of Young German Cinema, which would blossom in the seventies into New German Cinema, Kluge's film career began when his friend and mentor, the German-Jewish philosopher Theodor W. Adorno, recommended him to the legendary director Fritz Lang in the summer of 1958, some three years after Kluge made Adorno's acquaintance by sheer chance at a public lecture in Classics held in Frankfurt, Germany. After completing his doctorate in law in 1956, Kluge worked as an assistant to the board of trustees at the Goethe University of Frankfurt. After several years of work, the twenty-six-year-old grew disillusioned with this chosen career path in law and aspired to become an author. Adorno, however, a champion of literary modernism, cautioned his disciple against making the fatal error of taking up the pen when giants before him like Franz Kafka, Marcel Proust, and Samuel Beckett had already exhausted literature's capacity for innovation. Sent to Berlin to work as an intern on the set of Lang's first European-made production following his American exile in Hollywood, Kluge witnessed firsthand how Lang's vision for *The Tiger of Eschnapur* (1959) suffered under the directives of the film's domineering producer, Artur Brauner. Left with little to do other than act as Lang's go-between, Kluge whiled away his time in the studio's canteen writing stories that would eventually appear in his literary debut, *Attendance List for a Funeral* (1962, trans. 1966). Due in large part to Kluge's connections to Lang, his superior at the Goethe University Frankfurt, Hellmut Becker, and Adorno, who became the director of the Institute for Social Research in Frankfurt in 1959, Kluge quickly found himself in the company of a cadre of young West German filmmakers. These aspiring directors sought to bring to the Federal Republic innovative films on par with those from the New Waves of Italy, France, and Eastern Europe. In spite of his lack of filmmaking experience, in his capacity as a lawyer Kluge co-signed the Oberhausen Manifesto of 1962, which declared the death of "Papas Kino" and the birth of Young German Cinema; co-founded West Germany's first film department at the Ulm School of Design that same year together with Detten Schleiermacher and Edgar Reitz; and negotiated in 1965 with the Federal Ministry of the Interior for the creation of the Board of Young German Filmmakers, which financially supported new innovative cinema. Kluge's first feature, *Yesterday Girl*, debuted at the Venice Film Festival in 1966, winning the Silver Lion for best director. Kluge thus became the first auteur of Young German Cinema to achieve such an international seal of approval.

Historically significant for our understanding of *The Patriot* is Kluge's long-standing preference for heroines. This proclivity began with his debut *Yesterday Girl*, resurfaced in his second feature *Artists under the Big Top: Perplexed* (1968), and returned once again with *Part-Time Work of a Domestic Slave* (1973) after a brief period of experimentation with science fiction. The central importance of Kluge's female leads in these three early films continues not only with *The Patriot* but also subsequent films like *The Power of Emotion* (1983). In an interview on the occasion of the debut of *The Patriot* in Hamburg, leading actress Hannelore Hoger mused, "I don't think that [Kluge] would have thought up a male character for the film."[11] Asked about this in Angelika Wittlich's 2002 documentary *All Feelings Believe in a Happy Ending*, Kluge attributed his predilection to a quirky personal opinion: "I believe women have a wealth of experience that men don't necessarily possess in equal measure when they follow their social roles. This is just my opinion. It's not necessarily true. Let me put it this way: I trust women more. In this respect, the most decisive protagonists in my films are not men."[12] Kluge's admiration for women's experience and the trust he awards them may seem at first glance like a feminist position, but feminists of the seventies and eighties were anything but enamored by his inquiry on screen into the concept he called the "productive power of women."[13] Especially alarming was Kluge's aforementioned film *Part-Time Work of a Domestic Slave*, about the backroom abortionist Roswitha Bronski. For West German feminists, this film in particular turned out after careful analysis to be not just a continuation of the patriarchal system they fought to overturn but also the work of not so much Kluge the self-avowed comrade in arms but rather someone they unmasked as a well-intentioned sexist whose work disqualified his own socialist-leaning sympathies. Like the protracted tremors of an earthquake, feminism's criticisms of Kluge and his films followed him long after these charges were first leveled in 1974.[14] Even though some West German feminists later contended in conjunction with *The Patriot* that Kluge had learned his lesson and abandoned the idea of a particularly female mode of production, by the early eighties American feminists had joined the original fray of criticisms, claiming that Kluge's preferred cinematic forms—especially his own voice-overs—always undermined his heroines' agency.[15] At the turn of the decade, West German feminists went so far as to diagnose the root of the problem: Kluge's good intentions were marred by bad theoretical influences.[16]

It is precisely for these reasons why we must briefly reflect on Kluge's provocative title a second time before embarking in earnest on our march through *The Patriot*. Given both Kluge's deliberate preference for heroines and the trouble they've caused him, shouldn't we refer to *Die Patriotin* in English as *The Female Patriot*? Why continue to elide the original German title's feminine "-in" suffix as movie houses, newspapers, English-language scholars, and DVD distributors have done in the past?[17] There are at least two perspectives we may entertain on this crucial issue. On the one hand, we could argue that the gender lost in translation in the standard English-language title deflects attention away from not only the contradiction that Kluge's title evokes by feminizing a quintessentially masculine word but also feminism's valid criticisms of his intentions.[18] On the other hand, opting for *The Patriot*, while foregoing the nominal subversion in the German original, might still be able to retain the title's jolt when used, for example, to name queer subject positions as well as non-European geographies and histories; incongruity between signifier and signified can unsettle the rules of semiosis. While *The Female Patriot* is undoubtedly the historically more accurate translation of the German title, identity politics have advanced in the interim to complicate the binary tension that the alternative English title (like the German feminine suffix modifying the German masculine noun) conveys. In this respect, Negt and Kluge have argued in their own history of the public sphere that the mechanisms that once excluded women from the classical public sphere (the sphere of newspapers, books, and public schools) have given way to a new public sphere dominated by mass media. This consciousness industry is now intent on incorporating everything that was once considered private: women's labor, children, the working class, personal interests, and private fantasies. (Anyone familiar with Amazon's predictive algorithms knows this all too well.) If our objective is also to unlock what's still contemporary about Gabi Teichert's patriotism, then we must acknowledge that the exceptional status Kluge reserved for her gender is an artifact of the past. As we will see in the final section of the present essay, this becomes especially clear in *Orphea* (2020), the second installment of Kluge's trilogy made together with Philippine New Wave director Khavn de la Cruz, in which Kluge's essentialism is supplanted by gender performativity played out on a transnational scale.

The task before us must be twofold for newcomers and aficionados alike. We must first track the historical particularities and limitations that shape the female patriot Gabi Teichert and her historiographic pursuits. Secondly, we must throw into relief how the grounds for her obstinacy linger on, and then ask why the contemporary agents of resistance and the terrain on which they operate nearly half a century later must be quite different. For this second objective, we will compare at the close of this essay how Gabi haunts *Orphea*.

In pursuit of the first objective, this essay offers close analyses of the original film in order to flesh out the dialogue between its concrete narratives and abstruse conceptual logic. One aim of these close readings is to show that nothing is arbitrary in Kluge's montage; every shot serves the sequence at hand. Comprised of 791 shots assembled in a frenetic montage subdivided into twelve sequences, *The Patriot* embeds its story of Gabi in a rich web of visual and acoustic associations typical of the essay film.[19] Defined by pioneer Hans Richter as the visualization of thought on screen, the genre of the essay film falls short, however, of capturing fully the deft ways Kluge's film blurs the boundaries between storytelling and conceptual thought.[20] When he published the screenplay to the film just three months after the film's debut, Kluge also included over one-hundred pages of material taken from his and Negt's still unpublished manuscript for *History and Obstinacy*, as if to say that the film and their philosophy were cut from the same cloth.[21] While it will be essential to recognize how *The Patriot* did arise from the very same "shop floor," to quote one scholar, where Negt and Kluge's *History and Obstinacy* emerged, it is equally important to recognize that Kluge's film is not simply the cinematization of their social philosophy.[22] How best to approach the conceptually informed narrative embedded in radical fragmentation typical of Kluge's best films therefore presents a hermeneutic challenge. Contrary to other readings that selectively identify non-linear correspondences in *The Patriot*, the following account analyzes the film's dozen sequences in their order of appearance in order to retain a sense of the variety format called the "number dramaturgy" that Kluge adopted from circus performances for this and other later films. Unlike the artificial dramaturgy of opera, for example, that conveys a cohesive, subject-centered sense of time and action, the undramatic nature of the number dramaturgy used in *The Patriot* corresponds, on the one hand, to the fragmented and depersonalized qualities Kluge associated with alienated social life in late modernity.[23] These inauspicious conditions already do not bode well for Gabi's patriotic ambitions. On the other hand, by preserving a sense of the film's number dramaturgy in our sequential analyses we also stand to convey the film's formal resemblance to the station drama, one of German expressionism's dramatic innovations, which eschewed causality, continuity, and closure. With each subsequent sequence, we spectators encounter another more extreme facet of Gabi's intelligence labor that by the film's end falls short of changing history. *The Patriot* is, however, not solely about the patriotic history teacher Gabi Teichert who tries in vain to change the past. There's a bomb squad in a cellar besieged by Allied bombers, a social democratic political convention, an excursus on fairy tales, a fight between a father and son, and a police raid on rowdy youths at a department store, just to name a few of the film's many seemingly disparate stories. And in between all these many scenes as well as all the many stills, intertitles, musical accompaniments, and clips of found footage, there's the frame narrative in sequences 1 and 12 of Kluge's renowned talking knee.

Sequence 1: Gabi Teichert and Corporal Wieland's Wandering Knee

The sequence that opens *The Patriot* seems at first like a ruse. "Gabi Teichert," Kluge's unmistakable voice-over intones, "a history teacher in the state of Hesse, is a patriot." Whereas patriotic teachers may not be something out of the ordinary, Kluge's subsequent assertion surely invites head scratching. "That means she takes an interest in all of the empire's dead."[24] There have certainly been patriots who honor their country's veterans, but what exactly does it mean to be a patriot and take an interest in *all* the empire's dead? There is, however, no time to consider these questions during the roughly ten seconds we see the black-and-white headshot of Gabi and the film's fleeting blood-red title sequence. Gabi quickly vanishes from view, and in her stead the next fifty seconds offers a précis of what the voice-over means exactly by empire and its dead. Accompanied by an excerpt from composer Hanns Eisler's score to Alain Resnais's 1956 documentary *Night and Fog* about Nazi concentration camps, we see an excerpt from German Jewish filmmaker Curtis Bernhardt's 1930 film *The Last Company* showing the carnage from Napoleon's triumph over Prussian troops in the Battle of Jena-Auerstedt of 1806. A second cut shows a mere six seconds of grainy documentary footage from World War II. Were we not paying close attention, chances are we would fail to recognize the German antiaircraft artillery firing its guns heavenwards. There's much to unpack in these first sixty seconds. Far from accompanying these images of Germans at war, Eisler's soundtrack to Resnais's film about Auschwitz operates as an acoustic counterpoint to these visual bookends.[25] At the one end is Prussia's bitter defeat at the hands of Napoleon, which catalyzed Prussian reforms as well as a thirst for retribution that led not only to Napoleon's defeat at Waterloo in June 1815 but also the creation of the conservative German Confederation in 1815 and a liberal opposition that yearned for the foundation of a democratic German nation. At the other end of this historical spectrum is that very nation under siege in World War II. To reckon with the German empire's dead is thus to invoke not only those who fell while defending home and nation but also those whom that nation destroyed in its nation-building efforts. That the German empire's dead Gentiles are indexed visually while the Jewish victims of its Final Solution are evoked acoustically suggests that for patriotism to make good on its commitment to the empire's dead it must look, listen, and, what's more, put into relation what can and cannot be represented. An ethics of Holocaust representation briefly surfaces in the form of iconoclasm, only then to vanish, too. If Kluge's Shoah stories are any indication, this fleeting allusion suggests that the medium of film is ill-suited for Kluge to wrestle with the enormity of German guilt for the Holocaust.[26]

Rather than circling back to Gabi, the next cut takes us farther afield by introducing Gabi's foil, a talking knee. The knee first recites the eponymous poem by Christian Morgenstern:

> A lonely knee travels through the world
> It's just a knee and nothing else!
> It's not a tree! It's not a tent!
> It's a knee and nothing else.
>
> There once was a man in war
> Shot through and through.
> Only the knee remained unscathed—
> As if it were a holy relic.
>
> Ever since the lonely knee roams through the world.
> It's just a knee and nothing else.
> It's not a tree! It's not a tent.
> It's a knee and nothing else.

What appeared in Morgenstern's day like a case of nonsense poetry turns in Kluge's hands into something quite literal. Shifting from the third person in Morgenstern's poem to the first person, Kluge's voice suddenly shifts positions to assume the guise of the knee and explain itself. Set against a series of contrasting images depicting terrestrial finitude and planetary time, the cultures of mourning and the birth of the German nation out of war, the knee's ensuing monologue explains that it once belonged to a corporal named Wieland who perished in the Battle of Stalingrad in 1943. As foreshadowed in the Morgenstern poem, Wieland's knee not only survived its owner but has managed to roam the earth with the intention of "rectifying a few things" by talking for "all of Corporal Wieland," "because no one is simply dead when they die." It would be a basic misunderstanding, the knee goes on to explain, "to assume that the dead are somehow really dead." Even though it may seem like the knee is speaking for all the dead throughout human history when it boldly asserts, "we are full of protest and energy," Corporal Wieland's knee is, in fact, a German knee interested, like Gabi, in German history. The knee is, furthermore, entirely aware that its assertions probably seem nonsensical for its listeners. Take, for example, when he asserts that bits of every human being live on after their physical demise, that a person's wishes live on in these bits, that these bits are a part of a historical totality, and that these bits literally have to go to battle in order to speak. Yet no one in their right mind would dismiss the knee's final questions as trivial or unrealistic: "Who really wants to die? How can I escape the history that will kill us all?" In light of the accompanying images, including those of German prisoners of war rounded up following their defeat in Stalingrad (see fig. 5), it's not unreasonable to conclude at this early point in the film that the history in question is uniquely German.

Kluge begins *The Patriot* like a mystery film, albeit without any of the requisite suspense. Just six minutes into a two-hour film, sequence 1 provides a partial dramatis personae, but we have no indication yet what the nature of Gabi and the knee's relationship to one another is. Before we push onward to sequence 2, where Gabi's intelligence labor begins in earnest, we should recall, especially for readers and viewers new to Kluge, that his highly constructed film aesthetic already on display at the outset of *The Patriot* is rooted in his theory of realism. Realism doesn't necessarily come to mind when we think of Kluge, especially when we compare him to New German Cinema's other internationally renowned directors like

Rainer Werner Fassbinder, Werner Herzog, and Wim Wenders. Grasping the roots of Kluge's theory of realism can take us backward to his earliest declarations on the medium of film and filmmaking. We could consider, for example, his writings that grew out of the Oberhausen Manifesto of 1962; his reflections on the film school he helped establish at the Ulm School of Design; his seminal 1965 essay co-authored with Edgar Reitz and Wilfried Reinke entitled "Word and Film"; or his many essays packaged together in his 1974 anthology on filmmaking named after his 1973 film *Part-Time Work of a Domestic Slave*. Yet we also find an equally rich catalogue of salient cinematic principles in Kluge's eponymous book published only three months after *The Patriot* debuted in September 1979, in which he explains his unorthodox approach to realist filmmaking.

Alongside the screenplay to the film published in the book *Die Patriotin*, Kluge includes notes on method that scorn the single narratives typical of ninety-minute features. If the intention is to tackle the history of a country like Germany, then so much more is needed. "Not one story but many stories," he insists.[27] Additionally, he holds that fictional narratives always impede spectators' actual social experience. For this reason, Kluge advances a frenzied visual and acoustic montage, as we have already seen and heard in the first sequence of *The Patriot*. Executed not by Kluge himself but rather New German Cinema's most adroit film editor, Beate Mainka-Jellinghaus, montage in *The Patriot* undermines any and all facile oppositions between documentary film and the mise en scène typical of narrative cinema. The purported objectivity of the documentary needs the emotions and desires of cinematic fiction as much as cinematic fiction requires real historical conditions captured by documentary in order to counter its illusions of individuals capable of determining history. What montage affords film is what Kluge calls a "morphology of relations," an entire world of forms through which the otherwise invisible relations of social experience—an idea that he adapts from Bertolt Brecht—are to be rendered imaginable for spectators.[28] In this respect, Kluge has similarly argued that the most important feature of cinema is not the material that montage sutures together but rather its cut, the breaks between images that provokes the spectator's fantasy with questions like *What links German myths (i.e., fairy tales) with an old illustration of a coffin, castle ruins, and German POWs in Stalingrad?* (see figs. 3–6). What's more, montage pushes the human capacity for understanding to the brink of confusion while also plying it with points of orientation with which it may navigate its way through time and space. Only when conceived thusly can film aspire to what Kluge has long regarded as its bona fide "antirealist attitude."[29] This attitude is the answer to his

Figures 3–6. Clockwise from the top left: a person crawling up a castle's icy glacis from below—"a nightmarish image repeated in German myths" (*Die Patriotin*, 53)*; Caspar David Friedrich's *Coffin on a Grave* (ca. 1836); documentary footage of German POWs after defeat at the Battle of Stalingrad; bucolic castle ruins filmed from above in 1979. © Kairos Film.

* Here and in several other instances the figure captions contain quotations from Kluge's book to the film, *Die Patriotin: Texte/Bilder 1–6*. These will be indicated parenthetically by short title and page number.

pivotal provocation that "It must be possible to present reality as the historical fiction that it is."[30] This antirealism seeks to translate into the language of film what human beings have long done when they clown around (i.e., they mock power), dream (i.e., they look for an escape), or go on the attack (i.e., they turn violent). In other words, film imitates formally what people do when they "protest against an unbearable reality" with the hopes of either coming to terms with it or overturning it altogether.[31] Like Corporal Wieland's knee, Gabi Teichert is full of "protest and energy," insofar as she, too, resists the tragic trajectory of German history. And like the knee, she is intent on rummaging through history in an effort to find material to make it less catastrophic. For all their similarities, the knee and Gabi are ultimately worlds apart; while she toils among the living, the knee is ghostly, omniscient, undead, messianic.

Sequences 2–4: Worldly Modes of Knowledge Production— Archeology, Astrophysics, Politics, Folklore

What kinds of knowledge are capable of altering the course of a nation's history? Unlike historians who sift through archives full of books, manuscripts, or unpublished papers, Gabi looks in unlikely places in her pursuit of evidence capable of changing Germany's historical record. At the outset of sequence 2 (entitled "At the Telescope"), we find her heading out at night with a shovel in one hand and a notebook in the other in order to excavate corroborating evidence. After a night of digging, she peers into a telescope as if to suggest that the earth doesn't contain enough evidence of a less catastrophic and thus more patriotic course for German history (see fig. 7). Of concern in this sequence is, however, not so much the new bodies of knowledge suitable for Gabi's sought-after patriotism as the conditions such a successful search must meet before it even sets sail. Above all, Kluge's montage here presents us with what he originally advanced in his seminal semi-autobiographical story "The

Air Raid on Halberstadt on 8 April 1945" published before he made the film, namely the twin principles called "strategy from below" and "strategy from above."[32] Below and above don't refer to places so much as they mark diametrically opposed "positions in historical relations" of labor power that we should regard, respectively, as shorthand for laborers' survival strategies and capitalism's long-standing hegemony.[33] As Kluge tells it in the aforementioned story, hegemony accrues its force over spans of time that far exceed those of individual humans, whereas protest is very often of the moment. This is why we see other characters in this sequence like Gerda Baethe (taken from said story) and bomb disposal expert Willi Münch waiting helplessly in basements and bomb shelters while bombers above—the culmination of decades of technology and organized labor power—dump their industrially manufactured payloads in order to annihilate their targets below (see fig. 8). In other words, if history is what ultimately does us in in the end—as the knee explains above—then history and our individual positions vis-à-vis its deadly force are so disproportionate that the former invariably outmatches the latter. For patriotism to change history, it must aspire to nothing less than tipping these scales. What sort of intelligence labor can achieve such great heights?

Gabi's initial recourse to archaeology and then astronomy quickly gets philosophical, for it becomes clear that human beings lack the faculties necessary for perceiving the differences between above and below. What's more, there is the problem, as Kluge explains elsewhere, that regardless of what guise it dons, protest usually ends up distorting our "capacity to differentiate within reality."[34] This is why Kluge tells us at the close of *The Patriot*, "Most of the time Gabi Teichert is rather confused."[35] What's needed in such circumstances, then, is an organizational tool capable of awakening what filmmaker Hans Richter once called the human being's "badly trained sensibility."[36] Awakening is just as much "a question of relationality" as is Gabi's confusion, Kluge's voice-over explains. Not

Figures 7 and 8. *From left to right*: Gabi looking for patriotic history at an observatory; Gerda Baethe with her children during an air raid (strategy from below). © Kairos Film.

only the many wild juxtapositions afforded by cinematic montage in this sequence (e.g., bombers, a nine-month-old newborn, and a three-day-old puddle) but also the use of slow motion and time-lapse photography, close-ups and long shots, night vision goggles and daytime shots, as well as found footage and fictional scenes all contribute to the cinematic production of optically discernable distinctions. Compared to the distinctions that Kluge's apparatus affords within the span of this roughly twelve-minute sequence, Gabi's approach to making history more patriotic—she queries both the telluric and cosmic—suggests that she is at the very least aware of the fundamental conditions responsible for history's tragic outcome. That Gabi peers into a telescope indicates as well that she, like Negt and Kluge, is all too aware of the fact that little to "no work has been done" in order to develop the human beings' "remote senses" necessary for discerning the distant times and spaces "above" where "the big decisions in history" are made.[37] No matter how instructive cinema is for us spectators, the crucial task of tilting these conditions away from tragedy and toward a more patriotic history continue to confuse her in spite of her shrewd recourse to the telescope.

In light of their fragmentary structure and their highly conceptual subject matter, none of Kluge's works are ever hermetically closed entities. Not only do they always index previous works but they also very often recycle and repurpose precursors in ways that create a complex, seemingly endless web of connections. Before we advance to sequence 3, entitled "At the Party Convention," we would do well in light of Kluge's own intertextuality to indulge in a digression on Gabi's origins. It will make far more sense why she turns to politics after digging like an archeologist and scanning the heavens like an astrophysicist once we determine what brought her to this tipping point in her career in the first place. Gabi Teichert is not original to *The Patriot*. For those who already know the anthology film *Germany in Autumn* that Kluge made together with many other luminaries of New German Cinema like Fassbinder, Reitz, Volker Schlöndorff, and others during the harrowing events of late 1977, Gabi Teichert should already be a familiar face. What *Germany in Autumn* provides us with that *The Patriot* glosses over are the motivations for Gabi's protest, the effect of her protest on her profession, and, most importantly, the model after which she is fashioned. We first encounter Gabi in *Germany in Autumn* just as we do in *The Patriot*, namely standing in front of her bathroom mirror (see fig. 1). We are also told that what moved her were the events of the "German Autumn"—forty-four days involving the kidnapping of a West German corporate lobbyist, the hijacking of a Lufthansa passenger jet, the suicides of three incarcerated domestic terrorists, and finally the murder of that same lobbyist in an act of retaliation—that gripped the nation and threatened to turn the Federal Republic of Germany's young democracy into a police state. All this mayhem brings Gabi to doubt what she should teach in her history class. We learn of the second point of departure for Gabi's search for a more patriotic history later in the film when she reads about the troubling career of the three stanzas from Hoffmann von Fallersleben's "Song of the Germans." Written seven years before the failed March Revolution of 1848, only the patently liberal democratic third stanza from Fallersleben's paean—"Unity and justice and freedom / For the German fatherland! / Towards these let us all strive"—was recognized in West Germany.

To Gabi's surprise, however, the patently expansionist first stanza—
"From the Meuse to the Memel, / From the Adige to the Belt, /
Germany, Germany above all"—was retained at the outset of the
Weimar Republic when the song became Germany's official national
anthem. "What fairy tales my people tell!" Gabi exclaims in disbelief
that such lofty ideals were yoked to expansionist fantasies. Gabi
ridicules such ambitions by calling them fairy tales. As we've already
seen in sequence 1, German myths, a topic we shall return to in
earnest below, are associated early in *The Patriot* with nightmares
(see fig. 3). Unmistakable is how Gabi's quick resolve in late 1977
to change the way she teaches echoes Kluge's own antirealist
convictions. That her efforts to counter these disastrous myths and
fairy tales pedagogically meets with disapproval from her superiors
is due to the fact that her principal regards her concept of history
as pell-mell, to which she responds, "I try to see things in their
relationality." In order to break the cycle of violence stemming from
the long quest for German national identity, Gabi strives, in other
words, to think about history less in terms of causality and progress
than in terms of a historical ratio of material forces—in other words,
labor—that continually tips toward disaster, a ratio that at least in
theory could be shifted away from the brand of patriotism that long
propelled German history toward catastrophe.

Of the additional pieces of information about Gabi presented
in *Germany in Autumn* that significantly broaden our grasp of her
character in *The Patriot*, it is one scene in particular that helps us
conceptualize what exactly makes her patriotism exceptional. After
applying her lipstick in her bathroom as she does in *The Patriot* as
well (see fig. 1), a cut transports us to a long shot of a snow-covered
landscape awash in daylight (see fig. 9). With her spade slung over
her shoulder, Gabi treks through snowy fields and streams in pursuit
of a location to dig. As the sun sets, we see her from a distance,
flocks of birds flying overhead, as she sinks her spade into the snowy
earth and flings soil over her shoulder. A film about West Germany's

political downward spiral in the autumn of 1977, when that year's snow had yet to fall, *Germany in Autumn* features more than just this one wintery landscape. There is, for example, Alf Brustellin and Bernhard Sinkel's sequence about fictional director Franziska Busch, whose crew shoots a burning flag in a snowy park for their constructivist-style melodrama. In a subsequent interlude, we see a woman through the snow-covered branches of a tree—Kluge's voice-over identifies her as Frau Holle from the eponymous Grimms fairy tale—standing at a window and shaking a duvet (see fig. 10). And in Reitz's sequence, accompanied by a song from Franz Schubert's cycle *Winterreise*, an armed guard interrogates two lovebirds before they are allowed to cross the snowy French border into Baden-Württemberg.

Without ever mentioning it by name, all the many icy-cold scenes in *Germany in Autumn* evoke arguably *the* seminal critique of German patriotism in its infancy, namely Heinrich Heine's *Germany: A Winter's Tale* (1844).[38] Modeled after William Shakespeare's *The Winter's Tale* (1623), which was thought in Heine's time to tell a nightmarish story typical of fairy tales that nevertheless ends happily, Heine's satirical epic poem, written thirteen years into his Parisian

Figures 9 and 10. Two stills from *Germany in Autumn* (1977), a winter's tale, *from left to right*: Gabi treads through snow in search of the "basic principles of German history"; Mother Holle: "make my bed nicely and give it a good shake . . . then it will snow on earth."* © Kairos Film.

* See "Mother Holle," in Jacob Grimm and Wilhelm Grimm, *The Original Folk and Fairy Tales of the Brothers Grimm*, ed. and trans. Jack Zipes (Princeton, NJ: Princeton University Press, 2014), 82.

exile, tells of the poet's brief bittersweet return to the German Confederation, a reactionary place where the rule of conservative monarchs made it impossible for the liberal Jewish German Heine to call Germany home. If only, Heine mused in the introduction to his poem, the "heroic lackeys dressed up in their liveries of black and red and gold" (the tricolor donned in the Prussian struggle against Napoleon) were to embrace the unfinished humane ideals of the French Revolution—freedom, equality, dignity, reason, beauty, and happiness—and bestow them on all of humanity.[39] "This is the mission and the universal dominion that I often dream about for Germany when I wander beneath the oaks," Heine confessed, "this is *my* patriotism."[40] Deeply anti-nationalistic and humanistic, Heine's patriotism dreams of an alternative to the belligerent chauvinism brewing east of the Rhine just as much as Gabi Teichert does.[41] Even though Gabi is no exile, she nevertheless shares with Heine a "love of fatherland"—Heine calls it "foolish yearning" and it brings him, like Gabi later in *The Patriot*, to tears—that is imbued with one part critique and another part "wish."[42] Instead of praising the pedagogical power of the poet's pen in one breath and cursing the Prussian king's scorn in another, as Heine does at the close of his poem, Gabi first looks under foot and then to the heavens for the raw materials supporting another forgotten German history more patriotic in the enlightened sense Heine advances at the outset of his winter's tale.

Empty-handed following her initial foray into archaeology and astrophysics, Gabi alters her course in sequence 3, "At the Party Convention," by turning her sights to professional politics.[43] Filmed in grainy black and white in a style reminiscent of *cinéma vérité*, the sequence begins with shots of Hamburg's wind-swept harbor. Pedestrians and police officers trudge through the rain to attend the Social Democratic Party of Germany's annual party convention held in November 1977. Following an establishing shot of Gabi marching up the stairs of Hamburg's Congress Centrum, the camera shows her seated in the plenary session where SPD chairman Herbert Wehner, chancellor and SPD member Helmut Schmidt, and rows of SPD delegates are already in attendance. "If I may get back to the crux of my agenda," Gabi explains to a delegate unconvinced by her discourse, "the basic materials for history instruction in secondary schools are not worth distributing, not because there was never any moving German history but rather because it was so moving that it can't be processed in a positive way" (see fig. 11). Asked whether she thinks her entreaty will influence others, Gabi insists that if she believes she can change history then they can change it, too. "I expect from you that you'll disseminate this. That's why I came here because this here is the source." Gabi's plea to representative democracy goes nowhere fast. In between her few direct appeals to unconvinced delegates, we see attendees busy fulfilling their assigned roles in the name of affirming—as party chairman Wehner puts it—its social-democratic commitment to the German people: party leaders indulge in oratory bravado; delegates debate and form voting blocs; and party representatives report the majority vote to television journalists. What sounds like patriotism wants, however, no truck with Gabi's agenda, not necessarily because the matter at hand—the party's position on atomic energy—is inherently more important than her curricular agenda for public schools. To the contrary, Gabi soon realizes that her strategy of direct confrontation ignores party protocol requiring a main motion (*Leitantrag*) to be brought before the delegates and, what's more, overlooks the power play common among leadership and lobbyists that inevitably leads to compromise, concession, defeat, and disappointment on the side of the minority. It is a "false conception," Kluge contended in his Fontane Prize speech given just six months before the premiere of *The Patriot*, to think of "politics as a specialized field," yet this is precisely the impression that the party convention leaves on Gabi.[44] In the end, the political manifestation of the strategy from above ultimately prevails over Gabi's strategy from below.

Figure 11. Gabi photobombs a television interview at the SPD party convention. © Kairos Film.

If sequence 3 amounts to another dead end in Gabi's pursuit of raw materials for a more patriotic German history, then sequence 4, entitled "Totensonntag" (rendered best in English as "All Souls Day"), signals a radical jump back to the root of her patriotism, namely her wishes. From what we've established thus far, Gabi wishes to teach a more patriotic account of German history, one based on neither German nationalism nor its catastrophic outcomes. In a word, she wishes for a happy ending. Yet what we see and hear next has seemingly little if anything to do with these desires. In contradistinction to the preceding black-and-white footage, we first see Gabi in color again, peering into the camera. We then see a series of eight stills of vivid landscapes framed with an iris mask, the first of which is the world turtle central to Hindu cosmology. Kluge's voice-over breaks the silence and explains, "Human wishes assume many forms." Like many mythologies, Kluge begins with a creation myth before addressing creation's antipode, namely death. Accompanied by Jean Sibelius's tone poem "The Swan of Tuonela," the next illustration of a castle on a cliff high above a ketch sailing at night is followed by one of a "little *German* house" sitting along a stream (see fig. 12), and yet another of a reindeer-drawn sleigh passing a snow-covered Russian cabin. Two vignettes, one of a schooner trapped in ice and another of two brigs sailing in arctic waters, are then followed by an illustration of Herculaneum and Pompeii at the foot of Mount Vesuvius nearly a century before its fateful eruption. Once again, Kluge's voice-over explains, "A temple of the future, 16 B.C." The final thematically relevant image is that of two lovers flying on the back of a kind-hearted dragon. Although Sibelius's accompaniment continues—next we see an unmasked black-and-white image of a mother swaddling her child in a snowstorm—it would be prudent to pause and unpack these initial sights and sounds, especially as they obliquely set the stage for what other commentaries have unsatisfactorily chalked up to an undifferentiated "palette of wishes" floating around in Gabi's head.[45] If, however, we take Kluge at his word when he writes that "music binds everything together" and consider the basis of Sibelius's suite as our starting point, then we begin to fathom a string of thought-images that culminate in one of Kluge and Negt's most original contributions to contemporary thought, namely obstinacy.[46] According to Finnish folklore, Lemminkäinen of the *Kalevala* is tasked with killing a sacred swan swimming between Tuonela, the island of the dead, and the world of the living. If the world of the living is akin to a house, of which we see several nationally specific iterations in these still images, then the various bodies of water also depicted (seas, oceans, and streams) and the vessels traversing them evoke the passage that Lemminkäinen must traverse in order to win the hand of wicked witch Louhi's daughter. Although Lemminkäinen pays with his life for attempting to transgress the boundary between life and death in the name of

Figure 12. A German house at the edge of a stream: "The word 'economy' emerges much later from 'oikos,' meaning especially homey" (*Die Patriotin*, 88–89). © Kairos Film.

love, the *Kalevala* nevertheless resurrects its hero, as some myths are wont to do. In Kluge's abbreviated iconic retelling, it is a dragon that whisks him away with his lover. In short, what we hear is a Nordic fairy tale that ends happily.[47] What we see certainly ends happily, too, but what are we to make of all the many intervening houses—the German house, a Russian dacha, the Roman temple—where the living reside? If human wishes do assume many forms, is the Finnish happy ending that is musically synonymous with, say, German wishes associated with the house?

Before we even have the time to settle the matter regarding these houses, let alone ponder the realm of the dead in these sundry images, Kluge pushes us forward into very different mythical territory. We now see in black and white the aforementioned mother with not just her newborn at her breast but a second young child in tow, a flock of ravens, a dreary winter landscape full of felled trees, and a religious procession approaching a wayside cross (another two images from Romantic painter Caspar David Friedrich, whose work we saw already in sequence 1). Once again, Kluge's voice-over chimes in to narrate the German legend entitled "The Obstinate Child" from the Brothers Grimm's *Children's and Household Tales*:

> Once upon a time there was a stubborn child who never did what his mother told him to do. The dear Lord, therefore, did not look kindly upon him and let him become sick. No doctor could cure him, and in a short time, he lay on his deathbed. After he was lowered into his grave and was covered over with earth, one of his little arms suddenly emerged and reached up into the air. They pushed it back down and covered the earth with fresh earth, but that did not help. The little arm kept popping out. So the child's mother had to go to the grave herself and smack the little arm with a switch. After she had done that, the arm withdrew, and then, for the first time, the child had peace beneath the earth.[48]

Associated by folklorists with a thematic cluster of international folktales about divine reward or punishment, this gruesome Germanic fairy tale has for Kluge far more to do with the fundamental experience of expropriation. Expropriation, Karl Marx explains in the first volume of *Capital*, was a key process in the transformation of feudal Central Europe into an emergent capitalist society. To that end, those people bound to the land—slaves, serfs, and bondsmen— first had to be detached from the soil they worked on and then dispossessed of their own personhood so that they could operate as a "free seller of labour-power" on the wage labor market.[49] It is this second form of expropriation that is thematized in this legend. Less obvious from its English-language translation, the tale announces already in its German-language title, *Das eigensinnige Kind*, what discipline and punishment sought to strip the child of, namely its own senses (*Eigen-Sinn*). What's more, it makes clear that no matter how brutal the expropriation is, obstinacy lives on well after death. "It cannot be killed," Kluge and Negt explain in their reading of the story, "nor does it die. It merely *withdraws itself* inward."[50]

If the initial set of images in sequence 4 are framed by fantastic stories about life's triumph over death, then this second cluster of decidedly German stories tells of the German dead who continue to haunt the living. Subsequent footage bridging the beginnings of German nationalism and Gabi's search for a more patriotic history drive this distinction home. In particular, a scene from Bernhardt's aforementioned film shows a Prussian soldier who succumbs at the hands of a chasseur in the Napoleonic Wars. Another shows Gabi at home grading homework. Whereas the first reiterates the theme of death, the other recalls the mother's punishment of obstinacy in the Grimms' tale, insofar as Gabi "crosses out the mistakes" in her students' essays, as Kluge's voice-over explains, "even though the mistakes are the best thing about them." Although the remaining material from this sequence will certainly perplex viewers at first sight on account of its many seemingly disconnected themes—a Frankfurt cityscape (see fig. 30), an interview with a toy salesman in a department store, battleships anchored in Venice's San Marco basin, and humans at war in outer space—they all nevertheless transpose the tropes of old houses and sailing vessels seen at the outset into other more modern temporal registers (e.g., skyscrapers and spacecraft). If, as Kluge and Negt argue in *History and Obstinacy*, landlocked houses and the work performed within them are what makes German fairy tales and the transgenerational experiences they encapsulate distinct from Mediterranean or even Scandinavian myths featuring marauding heroes who find happiness, then what holds true about the images of various travels for German experience is their deadly outcomes.[51] This is the common denominator we should recognize in the story of the obstinate child, the subsequent excerpt of the fallen Prussian soldier, and the final illustration of the vanquished astronaut. This is also why German myths and the wishes they contain are so often "nightmarish" and unhappy and why they invariably repeat themselves long after their wishers are dead.

Sequences 5–8: Obstinacy and the Intrusions of Instrumental Reason

Obstinacy, Kluge and Negt explain, is "not a 'natural' characteristic, but emerges out of destitution. It is the protest against . . . the expropriation of one's own senses that interface with the external world."[52] Obstinacy is surely not an exclusively German characteristic. As Kluge and Negt point out, it finds one of its richest literary elaborations in the ancient Greek story of Antigone, the sister who refuses to abide by King Creon's law against mourning and proceeds to bury her brother Polynices. Like Antigone, Gabi is an obstinate woman who refuses to settle for the traumatic repetitions of German history that in the fall of 1977 brought West Germany's fledgling democracy to teeter on the brink. As established already in connection with sequence 2, obstinacy disorientates our powers of perception, and in Gabi's case this means that in spite of her feelings of protest against German history she inadvertently undermines her own position when she corrects her students' homework from the standpoint of the very historical narrative she wishes to challenge. (On this note, Kluge once explained in an interview, "There's something quite contradictory about being a patriot."[53]) What sequence 4 also fleshes out that sequence 5 goes on to address in greater detail is Kluge's Marxian concept of history. Thus far, *The Patriot* has associated history with capitalism's organization of labor, which culminated in Germany, on the one hand, in the machinery of world war and, on the other, in anti-capitalist terrorism. We also have established that history operates according to the hegemonic "strategy from above" and can only be adequately recounted using multiple narrative perspectives (including the "strategy from below").

When grasped through the optics of German fairy tales, however, history boils down to a matter of work or, to use the language of Marx once again, the mode of production characteristic of pre-industrial capitalism, which Kluge and Negt contend was long organized around the home.

The "mode of production"—Marx's *terminus technicus* for the confluence of human labor power, the means of production (i.e., capitalism's infrastructure), and the "relations of production" necessary for reproducing human life—is what gives rise to a community's legal and political superstructure, its social consciousness, and its material life. Following Marx's *The German Ideology*, Kluge and Negt recognize that social life in Central Europe was long organized around work performed in the home and that this mode shaped not only a regionally specific consciousness but also inadvertently spawned a chain of protest energies.[54] Furthermore, the house so central for the organization of labor promoted a lasting consciousness indifferent toward one's own labor capacities, ill-disposed toward the public sphere, and, most importantly, inadequate for barricading the home from outside threats. This is why German myths are more prone to address what Kluge and Negt call the "'how' of wishes": "How do I recognize my enemy at all? Where exactly lies the boundary between inside and outside, between safe and absolutely dangerous?"[55] Complicating matters even further, the role of the house in the history of Germany's modes of production found itself in the midst of a transformation right at that moment when Kluge made *The Patriot*. While Gabi grades her pupils' essays, the *Gründerzeit* apartment building next to hers is being demolished (see fig. 13), while Frankfurt's skyline accommodates new skyscrapers— banks where production revolves around financialization—built on top of layers of discarded manual labor accumulated in lost artifacts. Gabi's obstinacy faces an uphill battle on two counts: it must account for both the heritage of labor's organization and its contemporary metamorphosis.

Figure 13. Gabi grades essays at home while a bulldozer razes the house next door. © Kairos Film.

Understanding obstinacy fully as the response to capitalism's long and continued history of expropriation requires us to follow Kluge and Negt's lead and expand our understanding of labor threefold before fully grasping the significance of sequences 5 and 6. First, work is not just what we do just to pay the bills. It is also what lovers, families, and friends must engage in outside their professions in order to forge happiness in their private relationships. If "love politics," as Kluge and Negt call the work done in the name of our social bonds, is also a form of labor, then only a fraction of the overall work we do is, in fact, wage labor. It then follows, and this is the second point, that labor cannot be restricted to manual labor. As already established at the outset of this essay, there is also intelligence labor, which can manifest itself as science and technology but also as teaching, preaching, practicing medicine and law, and producing news on television as well. What all of this has to do with patriotism begins to come into view when we consider the use value of intelligence labor established at the outset of this analysis. If critical intelligence seeks to produce a public sphere, then Gabi's patriotism is a wish for a community capable of redeeming obstinacy's destructive repetition compulsions.[56] At the beginning and ending of sequence 5, entitled "Digging," we see Gabi and other hobbyists exhuming ancient vases buried under the foundation of a demolished house; Kluge's voice-over intones that what was once a commodity (and in turn is the result of labor power) is now a treasure suitable for a museum. Noteworthy, Kluge also points out, is how, in the age of Augustus, manual labor and the making of community were both bound to the land.[57] In the German Autumn, however, Gabi's intelligence labor and its relationship to the mass media-fueled public sphere are precarious, for they can claim no such solid footing. In discussion with a fellow digger, she discusses the legal ramifications of their scavenging. "So I'd lose my job?" she asks, were she to be caught. "That's something a public servant needs to worry about," he replies. Equally worrisome is Gabi's inability to speak up in a faculty meeting where colleagues defend, against their disapproving department chair, a materialist conception of history not unlike hers. If her next move is any indication, then Gabi's conviction in the efficacy of her professional intelligence labor and its attendant wish for engendering community has slumped. This is why we suddenly find her in an orthopedics lecture concerned with the cortical homunculus and the nervous system's asymmetrical relationship to the hand, the locus of manual labor, and the foot. Bound in shoes one's whole life long, the feet pale in comparison to the oversized role the brain awards the richly innervated hands. Gabi concludes that a whole realm of overlooked intelligence relegated to the feet could be marshaled in ways that circumvent the weaknesses of intelligence seated in the brain (see fig. 14). Unsurprisingly, her idea for "history as history of the body" meets with just as much disapproval from her superiors as her previous attempts at altering the course of history instruction in her classroom.

Figure 14. Gabi measures her roommate's feet, data for a history lesson on the body. © Kairos Film.

With sequence 6 we arrive at the midpoint in *The Patriot*, where Kluge's third qualification regarding labor is thrown into relief. Whereas sequence 5 ends with the disqualification of Gabi's case for a new history of the body, sequence 6 underscores the precariousness of her intelligence labor further by putting it into a much larger historical context. In addition to the two previously mentioned spheres of labor (private industry and intimate relationships), there exists a third significant sphere of labor that we perform on ourselves and that is necessary for balancing out the countervailing demands that industry and relationships place on us. If all goes according to plan and we succeed in offsetting the alienation of the former and the reciprocal conflicts of the latter, then we achieve what Kluge and Negt call a "balance economy of labor capacities." Yet aggressive forces from above continually threaten to sabotage this control.

Interspersed among intertitles, newsreel footage, still photographs, excerpts from silent-era films, and original footage of a father, District Attorney Mürke (Alfred Edel), and his son (Hanno Loewy) watching television, Kluge juxtaposes in sequence 6 three narrative vignettes. Common to all of them is the problem of state-organized labor and its attendant instrumental reason, which together interfere in other more private forms of social labor. What is lacking in each of this sequence's stories is balance.

The first cluster of scenes, which lends the entire sequence its title, "The Voyeur," begins with a close-up of a nameless middle-aged man (Dieter Meinka). "My professional tools are my eyes," he declares, "I'm interested in *knowledge.*" We then learn that he works for the department for state security and political crimes. In his free time, he deploys the very same professional tools to spy on unsuspecting women in various states of undress.[58] Unaware that his next victim, none other than Gabi Teichert, has caught him in the act, he peers into his binoculars while she sneaks up on him, but instead of her reporting him to the police they retreat to a café, where Gabi gives the discontented voyeur unsolicited advice: "A voyeur like yourself needs to relax!" The second cluster of scenes entitled "The Relation of a Love Story to History," tells of newlyweds Fred and Hildegard Tacke, who spend their first vacation in Mussolini's Rome on the eve of World War II. After they marvel at one another in front of their hotel's floor-to-ceiling mirror, Fred takes his leave of his wife to report to the German front (see fig. 15). Fourteen years later, he returns home after his internment in a Russian prisoner-of-war camp. "Now the two are expected to resume the love story from August 1939," Kluge's voice-over explains. In "The Song of the German Armed Forces," the third and final cluster of scenes, which was directed not by Kluge but by Margarethe von Trotta, a delivery man (Marius Müller-Westernhagen) drops off a brand-new television to be raffled off at an Armed Forces' mess hall. "I've always wished for a little television like that," says one officer. The

Figures 15 and 16. The labor of relationships, *from left to right*: newlyweds Fred and Hildegard Tacke (love interrupted by the labor of war, patriotic); soldiers (patriotic) serenade a television delivery man with a love song (love misplaced). © Kairos Film.

presiding officers express their gratitude by offering the young man a beer and singing to him Gerhard Winkler's 1942 hit song "Please Don't Worry about Me (A Letter from the Homefront)" (see fig. 16), a song that debuted in a request show on National Socialist radio for soldiers and their sweethearts. What these stories share with Gabi's is the incursion of one mode of labor into other. An intelligence laborer like Gabi, the state security agent in the first vignette fails to reconcile his two vocations and as a result suffers from insomnia. Similarly, the mass mobilization of German wartime labor in the second vignette puts the Tackes' labor of love on indefinite hold; whether their reunion succeeds remains a mystery. And in the third vignette, a love deferred because of war rings forth thirty-seven years later not via radio but rather on account of another medium, namely television, the new ersatz for German wishes. As a result, a random delivery man finds himself suddenly pulled into someone else's anachronistic love politics while just trying to do his job. In the second teacher conference with Gabi's principal and fellow colleagues, which begins the next sequence, we see once again that she, too, is no stranger to one kind of labor intruding on another. The disapproval she met with earlier has now escalated into threats of potential termination for anyone who dares politicize the classroom.

The strategy from above now manifests itself in the guise of state power (West Germany's Anti-Radical Decree), which threatens to quash the fledgling solidarity among her and her colleagues. Achieving a balanced economy of labor capacities is, in brief, easier said than done.

Where exactly lies the source that foils Gabi's efforts to teach a more patriotic history? In sequence 7, we learn that her meddlesome principal from sequence 6 is just a contemporary manifestation of a longstanding juridical precedent encapsulated in German fairy tales. After Gabi's second confrontation with him, at which point her powers of reason momentarily fail her once again, her obstinacy gains a second wind. Her next course of action entails a visit with Undersecretary Hans Heckel, the former superintendent of the Hessian school system, who shares with her his shrewd juridical analysis of the German fairy tales that Kluge's voice-over first introduced at the film's outset (see fig. 3). The tale "The Companionship of the Cat and Mouse," we learn, is really about racketeering, and "The Wolf and the Seven Kids" features not a big bad wolf but rather a mass murderer. If "fairy tales reverse real experience" as Kluge and Negt insist, then Heckel's commentaries about the extralegal ramifications woven into these and other tales lay bare how many German wishes conserved in these narratives are expressions of coercion.[59] Yet for all his insight into the "historical kernel" of fairy tales—fairy tales, we are told, tell how a people "works for over 800 years on its wishes"—when asked about his past professional accomplishments Heckel takes credit for creating the very same administrative "coordination" at Gabi's school that now forestalls her attempts at marrying her obstinate moonlighting with her day job as intelligence laborer who teaches history. The ensuing two-minute montage whisks viewers past references, among other things, to disasters both big and small from the two world wars (the Battle of Verdun, a senile President Hindenburg, Wehrmacht soldiers marching toward a Christmas tree) only then to conclude with a final color illustration of a cave that looks out onto a volcano erupting against the starry sky. "Whoever laughs at fairy tales was never in distress," Kluge's voice explains. By dint of the inverse relationship between the "strangely auspicious and joyful outcome[s]" typical of the Grimms' tales and the disasters of German history, we arrive at the outlines of an anthropological theory of fairy tales in the form of a single image (see fig. 17). In a word, fairy tales engender illusions of interior refuge safely removed from the mortal dangers waiting outside.[60] If Heckel's testimony is true, Gabi's chance at getting at this truth and, what's more, putting it to good use was foiled well before she ever entered the classroom. No matter how probing, her critical intelligence doesn't stand a chance against instrumental reason. After all these dead ends, her few remaining options grow more extreme.

Gabi's next move marks the beginning of her radical shift from the macro to the micro. In sequence 8, entitled "She Tries Her Hardest and Gets a Stomachache," Gabi turns her search on herself. Once again, Kluge's voice-over sets the stage, "The insides of a person who tries their hardest are like a factory, a workshop, a basement, or even a witch's kitchen." Interspersed between photos from Gabi's childhood, documentary footage of military executions, a bush near Kaliningrad, Willy Brandt's resignation, a fight between the aforementioned District Attorney Mürke and his son Theo, who is enrolled in Gabi's history course, and the story of fireman Schönecke, we see scenes of Gabi in her laboratory where she destroys books in pursuit of knowledge contained not in their content but rather in their substance. In the blue haze of her window-lit lair (see cover image), she first wields tools typical of manual labor: a pipe wrench, a sickle, a hammer, a saw, and a drill. Often thought of as depicting the extraction of German history's missing links from its master narratives, most telling about these iconic scenes from *The Patriot* is Gabi's resolve to imbibe a sweet concoction made by mixing torn-out pages from books and orange juice concentrate (see fig. 18).[61] If

Figure 17. "Whoever laughs at fairy tales was never in distress" (*Die Patriotin*, 129, 465). © Kairos Film.

Gabi can't change the history Germans have made, then why not change the Germans at the cellular level? Just as Kluge and Negt explain in *History and Obstinacy*, Gabi's stomach revolts against this imposition from on high.[62] While she is next seen consuming crackers and milk in the classroom to soothe her stomach cramps, her students complain that her teaching has suffered. "You need to try harder!" Theo implores. "Don't torture me," she retorts. "I've got a stomachache and I'm overworked."

Sequences 9–11: Natural History as a Constellation of Trees

Instead of interrogating the four sequences that conclude *The Patriot* separately as we have the others thus far, it will be far more productive if we first consider how one of the film's recurring

Figure 18: Gabi drinks a book in her laboratory. © Kairos Film.

"thought-images" culminates throughout the final quarter of the film in a constellation seminal for all of Kluge's cinematic thought, namely the utopia of film. For Kluge, utopia in the sense of a "good place" and a "no-place" manifests itself in the production of temporalities favorable for trigging the spectator's imagination. A cinema that neither contracts time using suspense nor expands time, as the strolling flaneur is inclined to do, is a cinema intent on making its spectators wait "for a better world," one "beyond the cinematic image."[63] An innovation developed by one of Kluge's most important philosophical influences, Walter Benjamin, the thought-image (also called the "dialectical image") was to be the cornerstone for an entirely different kind of history writing set on "brush[ing] history against the grain."[64] If history is indeed written by the victors, then brushing history against the grain seeks to recast history from the vantage point of those vanquished under capitalist relations. To this end, Benjamin proposed that his materialist historiography could unseat the empire of concepts like "progress" so central to dominant historicist paradigms and therewith unlock phenomenological alternatives to time and experience by allowing images to "'spring[ ] forth' from constructions of the historical material itself."[65] As Benjamin's *Arcades Project* makes clear, this raw material was to be culled from sundry *textual* sources arranged into constellations according to the principle of montage. The images themselves unfold not in the constellations but rather in the mind of their beholder. Although Kluge's theory and practice of cinematic montage appears to be cut from the very same cloth as Benjamin's concept of the dialectical image, what sets him apart from his mentor is his recourse to actual images, that regime of vision that the doyens of the Frankfurt School very often associated with the mass spectacles of fascism. When addressing the calculus of his cinematic montage, Kluge has repeatedly identified his role as filmmaker as that of an *artiste démolisseur* whose job it is juxtapose two images such that both cancel one another out and in the process give way to an imaginary third, film's approximation of Benjamin's "thought-image."[66] Yet Kluge's films are also richly appointed with kindred images that by dint of their recurrence don't so much fall away as persevere to form a meta-constellation in their own right. One such cluster of recurring images in *The Patriot* that culminates in the final quarter of the film is that of trees. First introduced in sequence 1 using a detail from Friedrich's painting *Oak in the Snow* (see fig. 19), images of trees are prominently featured again in sequences 2, 4, 6, 7, 8, 10, and 12. With each and every iteration, Kluge's trees acquire an increasingly more complex array of associations that index, as we shall discover, the bedrock of Benjamin's and Adorno's dialectical theory of history as natural history.

Trees are never just trees for Kluge but rather natural matter interpenetrated with human history. Take, for example, the ways in which the Christmas trees featured in sequences 4 and 7 link up

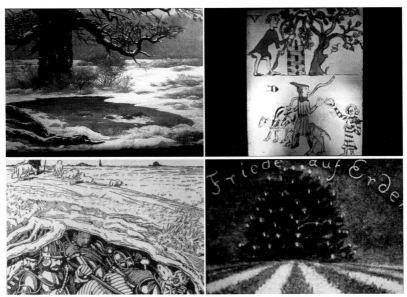

Figures 19–22. Trees of history, *clockwise from top left*: Caspar David Friedrich's *Oak in the Snow*, n.d.; a detail from the Heidelberger *Saxon Mirror*; "Peace on Earth": "An army of a million German soldiers marches in six columns" (*Die Patriotin*, 128); cover illustration of Clara Viebig's *The Sleeping Army* (1904). © Kairos Film.

with other trees in *The Patriot*. The first Christmas tree we see is juxtaposed against the illusory world of commodities (fashion, dolls, homewares) sold at the department store Kaufhof. This association with the logic of capital is later refracted through the illustration from the Heidelberg copy of the twelfth-century illuminated manuscript *Saxon Mirror* featured in sequence 10, which depicts a man exercising his right to chop down another man's tree that is encroaching on his property (see fig. 20). If private property is, according to Marx, the antithesis between labor and capital—"*private property* is," he surmises, "the necessary consequence of *alienated labour*"—then it is only the law and by extension the state that can adjudicate when the violation of this contradiction essential for capitalism doesn't count as theft.[67] What makes these and other historical interpenetrations of nature in *The Patriot* decidedly German becomes especially clear with the second Christmas tree in the black-and-white illustration featured in sequence 7 (see fig. 21), in which millions of soldiers march toward an illuminated tree framed by the words "Peace on Earth." From their *Pickelhauben*, the characteristic spiked German army helmet of the day, we can surmise the time to be autumn of 1914 when widespread German belligerence was stoked by assurances that the war would be over by Christmas. And if we recall the Christmas tree's precursors in Indo-Germanic mythology, e.g., the world tree Yggdrasil in the *Edda*, then the cover, shown in sequence 12, of Clara Viebig's anti-Polish novel *The Sleeping Army* from 1904, in which medieval knights sleep under tree roots, recalls (in one possible reading) Niflheim. According to Norse cosmology, Niflheim is that primordial realm of the dead ruled by the goddess Hel waiting in Viebig's fin-de-siècle context to rise up and claim the eastern Polish reaches of the Prussian frontier as their rightful German *Heimat* (see fig. 22).[68] Even though no there are no trees present in sequence 9, entitled "It's Christmas Time," the individual units in the semiotic chain capitalism–law–nation are set into motion when Gabi witnesses Frankfurt police cracking down on youths charged with disturbing the "Christmas peace" (*Weihnachtsfrieden*) at the aforementioned Kaufhof. "I'm the one here with the authority to enforce the house rules (*Hausrecht*)," the department store manager explains when asked about the use of police force. It turns out, then, that this minor incident in late 1977, when private property took recourse to the law in the name of defending Christmas peace— an illusion already exposed by the second Christmas tree image discussed above—is in fact made possible by more than 700, or 800, or even 2,000 years of alienated German labor organized around the idea of house and home.[69]

A full dialectical grasp of natural history must also lend credence to those portions of the natural world not yet assimilated by history, what Adorno equates with the "concept of myth." Furthermore, it must consider the ways in which history also appears interpenetrated by nature.[70] While the former find their clearest expression in the short black-and-white scene of a bush near Kaliningrad from sequence 8 (see fig. 23)—"This region was once known as Königsberg," Kluge's voice-over explains, "This doesn't concern the bush."—the latter is the subject of the opening scene in sequence 10, "Alpine Canals." Sitting in a circle with the few pupils still in her history course, Gabi reads aloud from a manuscript that, upon closer inspection, turns out to be Kluge's aforementioned story "The Air Raid on Halberstadt on 8 April 1945." Up for debate is the plight of schoolteacher Gerda Baethe trapped with her three children in a garden house with a partial cellar while the Royal Air Force drops bombs. "The last chance to defend oneself against the misery of 1944 was in 1928," Kluge first explains. "In 1928, Gerda Baethe could have organized together with other women." Yet District Attorney Mürke's son Theo raises doubts as to whether the matter of organizing labor to prevent future disasters is so simple: "You can't simply organize people and turn them into marionettes [. . .] Organization is essentially the question: how can I organize twenty-thousand people? That can only happen if I already gave these twenty-thousand people a consciousness about where they have to fight." The necessary consciousness for such a political organization of labor capacities arrives, however, too late, another student interjects. Given what we've established above, even a sixteen-year head start is not enough time to undo centuries' worth of capitalist relations. To grasp it dialectically, history must be understood as both a social mode of conduct capable of giving rise to "something new" and as what Adorno, following Georg Lukács, calls "second nature" or more simply "petrified history" devoid of any historical appearance.[71] What Gabi's students struggle with in this opening scene of the sequence is precisely the structural dilemma that precludes a strategy from below from ever standing a chance of effecting change. Capital's centuries-old processes of separation, expropriation, and accumulation that subtend the strategy from

Figures 23 and 24. *Left to right*: A bush near Kaliningrad (Königsberg); sketches for Organization Todt's alpine canals (which were never built). © Kairos Film.

above ensure that the catastrophes of history will repeat themselves again and again.

There are, however, consequences to the structures that lend history its mythical appearance. One is psychological in nature and another societal in scope. "If a person wishes for something hard enough," Kluge's voice-over explains later in sequence 10, "then it comes true." It was in their *Public Sphere and Experience* from 1972 that Negt and Kluge first established that, within a political economy of labor power, fantasy must be understood as that compensatory realm where our reservoirs of non-alienated labor toil to offset the otherwise "unbearable, alienated relations" of the labor process.[72] Fantasy is, in other words, "inverted" or false consciousness essential for the maintenance of the balance economy of labor power. As two ensuing vignettes suggest, wishes lead to either downfall or hubris. The first vignette tells of Luftwaffe pilot Dennerlein, who hopes to glide safely back to earth after his plane is shot down. "At 150 meters above ground, I'll let go," he says to himself, but if the image of his pulverized plane is any indication, his wish for survival never comes true. The other vignette tells of a nameless civil engineer from Hitler's Organization Todt who dreamt of building alpine canals for barges to travel from the North Sea to the Adriatic Sea (see fig. 24). Even though the alpine canal system was never realized, its architect remains convinced that his colossal project was feasible on account of his extensive organizational planning. In both scenarios, there is no lack of organization—ground crews beam their searchlights at Dennerlein in free fall with the intention of helping him—but the consciousness in question is entirely ensnarled in alienated reality. Like Gerda Baethe, the ninth-century farmers briefly featured in between these two vignettes have, conversely, no shortage of antirealistic consciousness. What they lack is the organization necessary for warding off the armed lords and their vassals who dispossess them of their land and livelihood. This mutually exclusive structural relationship between consciousness and organization framed by the unyielding relations of production brings us to the second consequence that gives the penultimate sequence its title, namely "Coldness."

Sequence 11 initially takes its cue from Adorno's philosophy of coldness but quickly opts for science instead in its pursuit of Gabi's previous shift to the micro. First broadcast as a radio address in the spring of 1966, Adorno's essay "Education after Auschwitz" contended that the objective conditions undergirding postwar German society were unshakable. This had in large part to do with the fact that the otherwise unconscious subjective social dimensions that once gave rise to the barbaric acts of Nazism and that continue into the present must be exposed so as to prevent people from committing genocide again. Technical rationality, the reification of the self, and social indifference are just a few of the features that Adorno associated with social coldness. Adorno opined that only critical self-reflection could possibly counteract this wrong state of things.[73] After seeing Gabi once again excavating artifacts buried beneath Frankfurt, we encounter her superintendent. A choker shot shows him smoking a cigarette and looking "pensive and skeptical" as he mulls over her poor "sense of order" and her insistence that it has nothing to do with any cold-heartedness on her part.[74] This momentary allusion to Adorno's language of social coldness is promptly jettisoned in favor of that other objective kind of coldness nowhere to be found in Adorno's call for a consciousness-raising pedagogy: next, we see a bourgeois domestic interior where District Attorney Mürke, his son Theo, and their guest (a military attaché) watch television; while transfixed by news coverage of the blizzard of 1978 in northern Germany, they discuss the difficulty of waging war in winter. Back in her witch's kitchen, Gabi uses a microscope to inspect helium atoms cooled to absolute zero. While she hums the melody to a military marching song, a researcher working in the laboratory next door explains the difference between ordered matter at zero kelvins and life at room temperature. Accompanying a black-and-white photo of the Wehrmacht's winter campaign at the Battle of Stalingrad in late 1942, Kluge's voice-over assumes the voice of the soldier digging into the frozen ground; not even explosives, he explains, proved helpful in their efforts to find cover (see fig. 25). Gabi then reenacts Galileo's famous gravity experiment to presumably confirm the laws of motion. Another scene from her classroom shows teacher and pupils alike in a catatonic state. An illustration of a house at the bottom of a lake is followed by the following poem:

> There once was a little man who was not smart
> who built his little house on a sheet of ice.
> He said: O, God almighty, let it always freeze
> otherwise I'll have to lose my house.
> As for the little house, it sank and
> the little man, he drowned, too.[75]

Concluding this montage sequence is a shot of Gabi in profile crying while driving her car (see fig. 26). Although we don't know yet the exact reasons for her sorrow, it would seem that her most recent discoveries have paralyzed her teaching entirely. The only conditions under which a reorganization of history is possible are conditions fatal for human life. "300 kelvins," Gabi's laboratory colleague

Figures 25 and 26. *From left to right:* The Battle of Stalingrad, "In the winter campaign of 1942 we tried to hack our way into the frozen steppe" (*Die Patriotin*, 159); Gabi cries while driving through the city. © Kairos Film.

explains, "separate the realm of the living from the realm where matter is ordered as best as possible." Whether it be in the home or on the battlefield (in the name of *Heimat*), ordering human labor power like helium atoms at absolute zero only leads to more tragedy.

Sequence 12: Relationality between the Living and the Dead

The final and longest sequence in *The Patriot*, sequence 12, "New Year's: Ode to Joy," begins with an intertitle and an implied question: "A Question of Relationality. . . ." We've encountered so many countervailing thought-images thus far that it's worth asking: relationality of what exactly? Is it the relationality between consciousness and organization, or labor and private property, or history and obstinacy, or the strategy from above and the strategy from below? If Gabi's penultimate object of study is any indication, then the relationality in question moves her search from the material to the metaphysical plane. The objective conundrum discovered in sequence 11, namely the impossibility of life in states in which matter is absolutely ordered, brings her to listen to the choral finale from Beethoven's Ninth Symphony while parsing those stanzas from Friedrich Schiller's poem left out of the libretto (see fig. 27).[76] "'There, through the cracks of coffins torn apart, / she stands in the chorus of angels,'" Gabi reads aloud while her roommates sing the very same lines from stanza five to Beethoven's unmistakable melody. "Who stands there?" she then asks aloud. Lost in their singing, her roommates fail to respond. Gabi quickly circles back to the ode's title and says, "Joy," but this obvious answer must surely leave her puzzled, for was she not in despair not long ago? After reading from stanza seven—"When the sparkling wine makes the rounds, / let its foam reach the heavens"—she asks in disbelief, "What's that all about?" Why Gabi turns to literary hermeneutics has very likely to do with the magical powers of unification articulated in Schiller's reworked first stanza that begins Beethoven's collage:

> Joy, bright spark of divinity,
> Daughter of Elysium,
> Fire-inspired we tread
> Thy sanctuary!
> Thy magic power reunites
> All that custom has divided;
> All men become brothers
> Under the sway of thy gentle wings.[77]

> [Freude, schöner Götterfunken,
> Tochter aus Elysium,
> Wir betreten feuertrunken,
> Himmlische, dein Heiligtum!
> Deine Zauber binden wieder,
> Was die Mode streg geteilt;
> Alle Menschen warden Brüder,
> Wo dein sanfter Flügel weilt.]

An ode to the ecstatic joy found in friendship, Schiller's poem harnesses what Friedrich Nietzsche would call roughly a century later the Dionysiac impulse, capable of dissolving all differences and divisions among humankind. What proved impossible in her laboratory, namely the unification of "the realm of the living" with

Figure 27. Gabi and her friends analyze stanzas five and seven from Schiller's "Ode to Joy," not included in Beethoven's chorus. © Kairos Film.

the realm of dead (where matter exhibits a maximum amount of structure), suddenly becomes possible through song. The imagined community of brothers in Schiller's poem finds its real equivalent as a sisterhood assembled in Gabi's shared kitchen. Yet this community is far from absolute. As Adorno points out in his own reading of the second stanza, Schiller's bourgeois utopia excludes anyone who knows nothing of true love or cannot claim a soul as their own. In Gabi's case, it is her unceasing intelligence labor that precludes her from joining in the revelry. From Adorno's perspective, there is little difference between Gabi's sisterhood and Schiller's "bad collective," for both produce the exclusionary conditions from which an outsider's loneliness and sorrow arise.[78] Might then the reason for Gabi's breakdown at the end of sequence 11 lie in her sudden realization that the wish for community, which originally motivated her pursuits, excludes her from that very community?

Doesn't her search for a more patriotic German history ultimately alienate her students? Doesn't Gabi's obstinate labor divorce her from her colleagues and superiors? "In such a company," Adorno asks of Schiller's bad collective, "what is to become of old maids, not to speak of the souls of the dead?"[79] If Gabi has come to terms with the consequences of her radical patriotism since her breakdown in the car, then it is the unanswered second half of Adorno's question— i.e., the status of the dead and their relationship to the heavens— that informs her intense interest in the fifth and seventh stanzas of Schiller's poem, for it is there where she begins to anticipate what Corporal Wieland's knee already knows when it later says: "*We are history*, the dead and every one of our bits and pieces . . . Every cell in every body that never wanted to die knows everything ranging from the beginning of the occident to the stars as well as how it all ends. The only one who doesn't know this is our cantankerous brain." The question of relationality is manifold, yet here it is the relationality between the living and the dead that is of central concern.

As Beethoven's majestic chorus continues, we see another complex montage, including verses by schizophrenic Austrian poet Ernst Herbeck, a photograph of a prisoner looking through his window, yet another two Christmas trees blowing in the wind, and a scene of the Cologne cathedral and the Hollenzollern Bridge at night. Lodged in between is a quote Austrian fin-de-siècle author, satirist, journalist, and playwright Karl Kraus wrote in 1911: "The closer you look at a word, the farther away it looks back." Several seconds later, the word "Germany" fades in, and then suddenly the music stops (see fig. 28). Once invoked by Benjamin to illustrate his theory of aura presented in his seminal essay "The Work of Art in the Age of Its Technological Reproducibility," Kraus's aphorism deployed here has arguably little to do with a general theory of artworks or a grand narrative about German history.[80] Rather, it describes the trajectory of Gabi's search. With each and every jump, her quest finds itself increasingly removed from her starting point. In her

Figure 28. Karl Kraus: "'The closer you look at a word, the farther away it looks back': Germany" (*Die Patriotin*, 129, 165, 353) © Kairos Film.

search to extract the raw materials necessary for a patriotic version of German history—i.e., a history that doesn't play into the hands of a nationalistic political economy of labor power that destroys those very raw materials—Gabi tries her hand at a series of disciplinary approaches that appear to get her closer to those raw materials but ultimately take her farther afield from her immediate goals.[81] From archaeologist to astronomer, from political activist to folklorist, from cryogenicist to philologist, Gabi's path finally delivers her to the doorstep of theology, for the dark corners of Schiller's poem suggest that the constitution of community that Gabi really wishes for must burst open coffins and summon the dead in order to recover those raw materials capable of brushing history against the grain. In this respect, it should come as no surprise that after a long absence the voice of Corporal Wieland's knee returns at this juncture to say, "If everyone is speaking, then I don't want to remain silent. A few things look somewhat different from the perspective of a dead knee." Dubbed over footage of battlefield carnage taken from Bernhardt's *The Last Company* that is also used in sequence 1, the knee's monologue goes on to declare that its dead cells know everything, and for good reason: "The resurrection of the dead," it explains, "presupposes the most fundamental knowledge of history." No matter how hard Gabi the intelligence laborer works, only a "magic power" could help her transcend the limits of her postlapsarian standpoint and lay claim to a knowledge on par with divine omniscience capable of bringing the dead back to life.

It should come as no surprise at this late point in our discussion that the knee's remarkable talk of resurrection is modeled after Benjamin's philosophy. For Benjamin, the idea of *apocatastasis*, or the restoration of all things to their primordial state, was not theological so much as it was political. In his *Arcades Project*, for example, he imagines *apocatastasis* as the urgent remedy for Marxism's many lacunae (e.g., its unexamined faith in progress). By redeeming every facet of humankind's past (even lost utopian moments, no matter how "minor"), *apocatastasis* could in theory put the fullness of the past to use for future "revolutionary action" and "revolutionary thinking."[82] "Marxism has no meaning," one Benjamin scholar explained in this respect, "if it is not, also, the heir to—and executor of—many centuries of emancipatory dreams and struggles."[83] That Gabi's present has utterly failed at putting its past to revolutionary— let alone political—use is punctuated in this final sequence, when we encounter a 1932 illustration of a utopian city, in which the agrarian labor required for its Babylonian-like hanging gardens exists side by side with white-collar laborers (see fig. 29).[84] Nowhere in all the many shots of contemporary Frankfurt's sterile skyscrapers interspersed throughout *The Patriot* do we see any such incorporation, let alone recuperation, of older forms of labor bound to the land (see fig. 30).

Figures 29 and 30. *From left to right:* "How a utopian metropolis will look in 50 years (illustration from 1932)" (*Die Patriotin*, 170); one of many shots of Frankfurt's skyscrapers (sequence 4). © Kairos Film.

The knee signals the political dimension of its own call for *apocatastasis* with its allusions to Lenin. After telling more about its deceased owner, the range of its motion, its interstitial location between thigh and shin, and its experiences in the final days of the Battle of Stalingrad, the knee asks not once but three times, "What is to be done?" Documentary footage of German tanks engaged in battle over a simple countryside house cut abruptly to black-and-white photographs of domestic interiors: a dining room, a kitchen, and an office with not one but three telephones (see fig. 31). "This is the furniture in Lenin's apartment," the knee explains. "What is to be done? Charge en masse in the form of a dead knee? Or disguise oneself?" An obvious allusion to Lenin's seminal text of 1902 *What Is to Be Done?*, the knee's questions are no less political than Lenin's. However, the knee clearly opts out of Lenin's organizational protocol for achieving the revolutionary consciousness necessary for advancing the working class as vanguard fighters of social democracy. "From the standpoint of a dead knee," it explains, "it needs to be said negatively. Don't ask, *What is to be done?* Instead, ask, *What won't I do?* If my cantankerous brain says, *Do that!* then I know what not to do. Instead of running, I stumble." Nothing less than a call to obstinacy, the knee's recourse to a politics of refusal is nevertheless no prescription for revolution, if we consult Kluge and Negt's own Lenin-inspired adage: "Revolution takes place when those below are no longer willing and those above no longer can."[85] If those above are grasped not as individuals with identities but rather as those cells involved in cognition, then the knee's passing non sequitur— "the transformation of all relations is a perception"—delivered in tandem with the image of Lenin's office full of phones suggests that a media revolution stands to alter consciousness. If this revolution didn't already happen in Lenin's own age, then it certainly has in Gabi's own, when the television infiltrated the home (see fig 32), the political convention (see fig. 11), and became the object of everyday wishes (see fig. 16). As Negt and Kluge already made clear in their first collaboration, *Public Sphere and Experience*, those laboring above have become industrially organized, leaving those laboring below with little chance to tip the scales toward revolution.[86]

If the preceding scenes indicate that in an age dominated by mass media political *apocatastasis* can only proceed negatively, then it would follow that Gabi's search for a positive outcome is doomed to failure. In fact, Gabi's engagement with the science of coldness in sequence 11 foretells a mutual exclusivity that sequence 12 affirms

Figures 31 and 32. The consciousness industry in the home, *from left to right*: Lenin's telephone room, "obviously the most important room" in Lenin's apartment (*Die Patriotin*, 173); District Attorney Mürke, his son Theo, and military attaché F. von Bock watching television in the Mürke's living room (1978). © Kairos Film.

with its juxtaposition of Gabi and Corporal Wieland's knee. The living (Gabi) and the dead (the knee) never enter into a cohesive relationship with one another.[87] In spite of their shared interest in history, the transformational knowledge Gabi so obstinately searches for is knowledge that the omniscient knee doesn't need (because it already possesses all that there is to know), and the knee's negativity (obstinacy that persists after death) is not enough to bring about a revolution among the living if those above are in lockstep with the consciousness industry. When seen in this light, it is not surprising that the film's ending has rung hollow for some critics.[88] After seeing Gabi once again at the SPD party convention, outside her apartment surrounded by bulldozers, in her classroom, and in the streets of Frankfurt, we find her one last time at home looking out her window at an unusual winter thunderstorm in the middle of the night (see fig. 33). The trees in her inner courtyard sway in the wind. We hear the growling of thunder. Light from inside her apartment illuminates the snow-covered branches until a bolt of lightning suddenly turns night into day (see fig. 34). Kluge's voice-over explains, "Every year on New Year's Eve, Gabi Teichert sees 365 days before her. Thus, the hope arises that she can improve the raw material for history classes in high schools this year." Why this hope after all the many dead ends and despair?

Figures 33 and 34. Nighttime, *from left to right*: "A winter storm. Heavy snowfall. Thunder, lightning. Seen from Gabi Teichert's window" (*Die Patriotin*, 178). © Kairos Film.

In his preface to his book to the film, Kluge insists that it, like the film, which immediately preceded it, is ultimately about a simple wish. In conjunction with the film, he once called it a "wish for community."[89] In his book, he calls it "cooperation."[90] Think of "David and Goliath," he adjures. "How associative must human forces be for a David to come into being who is capable of shooting the monstrosity called reality in the eye. That is the question."[91] Like the collaborative film *Germany in Autumn* that came before it, *The Patriot* originally adopted cooperation as its guiding star. Kluge sought to enlist Herzog, Hans-Jürgen Syberberg, and Fassbinder, along with a handful of documentary filmmakers, but only von Trotta delivered her promised short.[92] Although the original vision never materialized, Kluge insists that the creative labor that went into making *The Patriot* was nevertheless collaborative. Based on an idea developed together with cameraman Günther Hörmann and actress Hoger in the wake of the Landshut hijacking, *The Patriot* eschewed what Kluge dismissed as the "screenplay fetish" and instead grew organically out of ideas advanced spontaneously by its editor Mainka-Jellinghaus, its actors, and its production team.[93] Yet even this collaborative mode of production on the set and at the editing table fell short for Kluge. "If you want to continue auteur cinema," he notes in his programmatic notes to the film, "then there's only the way of cooperation. Everyone is the author of their own experiences. They are not department store managers of their experience."[94] Contrary to a culture industry that sees moviegoers as entrepreneurs of their own experiences, Kluge extends collaboration outward to include his spectators, who must also work at turning the messy spectacle of *The Patriot* into an experience with broad and deep social significance. Accordingly, if Gabi's patriotic search ultimately boils down to a question of relationality, albeit a non-cohesive one, then this search must play itself out not only diegetically but also in the minds of Kluge's spectators. Kluge has long insisted that cinematic montage traffics in the language of relationality.[95] Only when this language is pieced together morphologically in such a way that it surprises its audience so much that it confounds their quotidian powers of perception and comprehension can cinema fulfill its utopian potential of making something unrealizable imaginable.[96] So when we witness Gabi at the close of *The Patriot* apparently at ease watching something as unusual and surprising as thunder and lightning during a winter night-time snowstorm, we should recognize that she is occupying a spectatorial position not unlike our own. To be sure, there is more at work here than just the play of light and the roar of thunder. That the object of Gabi's gaze is a tree is no coincidence. As we have already established, all the many trees throughout *The Patriot* index that dialectical approach to history, namely natural history, advanced by Kluge's Frankfurt School mentors Benjamin and Adorno. Whereas many of the film's trees invoke history as the unalterable catastrophic product of alienated labor, this last scene (of Gabi watching the flashing image) of a tree encapsulates how the spectacle of cinema can engage a collective in imaginative labor (at the very least, we watch Gabi watching). It is this cinematic arrangement that is in theory capable of exposing the ahistorical nature of history (by bringing it into consciousness) and kindling hope for "an alternative history in the future" (secure against the forces of capital).[97] Gabi's hope for the new school year will only seem naïve or misguided if we overlook the fact that the labor for such an alternative history is already bound up in the collaborative labor capacities activated when we watch a film like *The Patriot*.

From Antigone to Orpheus

In contradistinction to the critical mass of scholarship on *The Patriot* that has singled out the question of history for analysis, the foregoing discussion of Kluge's film maintains that its actual emphasis lies on labor. Why is German history full of oppression, strife, war, suffering, and needless death? Because many Germans made it that way, though not because they all chose to, but rather because many toiled for centuries under structural conditions that were unstoppable. What is it about the dominant mode of production under capitalism that made German history catastrophic over and over again? An unavoidable consequence of life under capitalism, the alienation of one's own labor also begets obstinacy, the cellular seed of all resistance and one of at least two conditions for revolution. In the case of schoolteacher Gabi Teichert, this obstinacy sparks off her search for a more patriotic (read: less catastrophic) German history. In *History and Obstinacy*, Kluge and Negt devote surprisingly little space to explicitly elucidating their concept of obstinacy. They parse the aforementioned Grimm brothers' fairy tale "The Obstinate Child," consider the tale of little Meret in Gottfried Keller's nineteenth-century novel *Green Henry*, and in closing turn to the story of Antigone.[98] There are indeed some similarities between Gabi and Antigone (for example, their disregard for the rule of law and their care for the dead), but there are also significant differences. Unlike Antigone, who is buried alive for her transgressions, Gabi will live another year with the hope that her wish will eventually come true. If there is a mythical antecedent to Gabi, then it is surely a composite including but not limited to Antigone. Other figures from Greek mythology like Odysseus and Heracles, two heroes who have loomed large in the imagination of other Western Marxists, come to mind on account of their adventures to the underworld.[99] Yet it is Orpheus's cause that is arguably the closest to Gabi's, for unlike these other heroes whose task it is merely to survive their passage through the underworld, Orpheus is the one who sets out to bring the dead back to the world of the living. What Orpheus dares to do in the myth is scientifically proven in sequence 11 of *The Patriot* to lie well beyond Gabi's grasp. In the ensuing four decades since the making of Kluge's film, however, transhumanist futurists, venture capitalists, and technologists have designated *anabasis*, or the return from the underworld, as something humans can actually attain. Gabi's eschatological dilemma has, in other words, become the latest facet of human experience to fall prey to the latest stage of capitalism's powers of absorbing everything into its clutches.

On the question of just how dated his film is, Kluge has agreed that the object of Gabi's late twentieth-century patriotism does indeed look different in the twenty-first century. Patriotism akin to hers must acquire new loyalties. Above all, it must ally itself with those particularities that stand in opposition to capitalism's centripetal forces of centralization while nevertheless promoting the very same wishes that guided Kluge's film *The Patriot* and the accompanying book, namely cooperation and community.[100] It should come as no surprise that in this respect Kluge follows Marx, who explained the process of centralization as following the law of "attraction of capital by capital" such that the result "grows to a huge mass in a single hand in one place, because it has been lost by many in another place."[101] The place that Kluge has associated in recent years most often with the centralization of capital in the new century is not Germany but rather Silicon Valley. Referring to the story of Odysseus, he has repeatedly called the hi-tech industry concentrated around the San Francisco Bay area today's "new sirens," "mythical creatures lurking on the perilous reefs of Silicon Valley." "Information technology," he insists, "understands our desires better and more rapidly than we ourselves are able to acknowledge or nurture."[102] As a result, these technologies leave us powerless against their countervailing powers, which are capable of assimilating some of the libidinous forces teeming within us while excluding many others.[103] As anyone who is familiar with—if not already proficient in—social media already knows, the centralization characteristic of digital (i.e., algorithmic or platform) capitalism has made both cooperation and community hallmarks of their interfaces. Yet what might seem like fulfillments of Gabi's wishes emerge from a contradiction, for the cooperation and community that Silicon Valley facilitates devastate the interiority of the individual where the particular resides. "Vast alien organizations," Kluge writes, "suck into their networks . . . the indigenous tribes residing within us."[104] What Silicon Valley embodies for Kluge, in other words, is a threat to what makes us particular. "What makes me particular," Kluge and Negt explain in *History and Obstinacy*, "is what I would not sell for any price," like, for example, "my dignity, my acre of land, my wife."[105] Community is therefore not a simple agglomeration of individuals. A person's particularities—their characteristics, personal property, and intimate relationships—constitute an inner community that enters into negotiations with an outer community also known as society. As we saw with Gabi's various engagements with German history, the expropriation of the former by the latter is what gives rise to obstinacy. For a community of selves ever to emerge, my own community comprised of multiple particularities organized economically around my home must negotiate with the communities of others situated in their own homes. Suffice it to say, Silicon Valley has rendered such negotiations rare, at best.

What would it mean then to transport Gabi Teichert—"a patriot of her own labor" who takes an interest in the German empire's dead—into our present-day network society?[106] Whose dead would captivate her patriotism? Who among the living would be included in her wish for community? What forms of labor would be necessary for her patriotism? What sort of dwelling would serve as the point of departure for her labor? Viewers of *Orphea*, the second installment in Kluge's trilogy made together with Philippine director Khavn de la Cruz, will instantly recognize from its title sequence its thematic affinities to *The Patriot*.[107] Subtitled *Apokatastasis pantōn*, after G. W. Leibniz's 1715 fragment on the restitution of all things, the film begins with title cards announcing such familiar themes as "bringing back all the dead," "lost utopia," and "the underworld" before launching into the story's image-driven exposition. Conceived in the traditions of the musical film and the rock opera, *Orphea* reimagines the Orpheus myth with which Jacopo Peri's *Euridice* (1600) heralded the beginning of opera. "There are something like 88 different Orpheus operas," Kluge once explained, but "the story always ends up the same."[108] In order to break this spell, he and Khavn found inspiration in Bob Dylan's 1965 song "She Belongs to Me" about a woman artist who "don't look back." In Kluge and Khavn's story, the myth's tragic hero is exchanged for a musically gifted heroine, but only after her former self, named Eurydice, dies and is reborn as Orphea. Played by Lilith Stangenberg, Orphea sings her irresistible music at bacchanalia held in Manila's slums, and falls in love with Eurydico, the son of Apollo and Nosferatu once known as Orpheus, who now works as a gay male prostitute in a Russian bordello in Manila (see fig. 35). Alternating between Khavn's punkish mash-up of eclectic footage shot on-site in Manila and Kluge's unmistakable montages of still images, intertitles, and performances by Orphea shot before a green screen, the film's loose non-chronological narrative is organized around her "nine love songs from hell" sung in English, Russian, Italian, and German. After demonstrating her musical powers by turning bordello clients into dolls, we see Orphea practicing her craft (tangos, arias, pop songs) and soon discover that she is also an adherent of biocosmism, that late nineteenth-century Russian movement committed to creating total state-controlled biopower by conquering human mortality through technology.[109] After learning of Eurydico's premature death, she sings her way into the underworld in order to negotiate for his return. Told in Tagalog that she has no business being there, she's sent away and is finally ejected from the underworld by the queen of the lice. Having returned empty-handed to the land of the living, Orphea sings, "I cry for someone else, I cry for ten cents, I cry for myself, I cry for poets." With her lament for the whole world in which everything has a price, Orphea pivots back to the macabre science of biocosmism while nevertheless devoting her song to suffering everywhere. At the film's close, a procession of the dead waits to cross back over the river Lethe. Whether Orphea's biocosmism triumphs over the

Figures 35 and 36. *From left to right*, from Kluge and Khavn's *Orphea*: Two lovers, Eurydico and Orphea in the streets of Manila; Orphea as biocosmist with hammer (with surgery projection behind her). © Kairos Film.

inevitability of all human death seems doubtful, however, as the line of those waiting to cross the Lethe remains at a standstill.

What exactly from *The Patriot* survives in the new guise of *Orphea*? What is historically different? What is new? Some of the most visually obvious overlaps between the two films occur when Orphea the biocosmist wields hand tools and eats torn pages from books in her "workshop for the resuscitation of the dead" (see fig. 36). Just like Gabi's search for raw materials for a new German history, Orphea's own quest for human immortality involves manual labor that assumes, however, fantastic if not grotesque proportions, especially when we discover that her workshop contains piles of corpses (including Eurydico's), hanging fetuses, and severed heads (including her own at one point) (see fig. 37). In his aforementioned Fontane Prize speech given months before *The Patriot* debuted, Kluge lauded works of art committed to telling stories about how abstract social conditions dictate and even destroy concrete human lives. In order to be successful, such works require tools capable of bringing abstract forces into perception. "I suspect that [the hammer and sickle] are tools," he mused, "which you can't do much with, either for the relation between people or for social experiences."[110] When considered in this light, not only does Orphea share with Gabi a tendency to misrecognize the perceptual tools required for throwing into relief—let alone reversing—hegemonic abstractions, but she (like Gabi) is also confused about, if not wholly unaware of

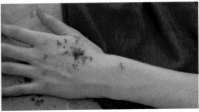

Figures 37 and 38. *From left to right*: Orphea, decapitated, in her workshop for the "resuscitation of the dead"; ants crawling out of Orphea's hand. © Kairos Film.

the forces she's up against. In fact, only once we tender a plausible explanation for Eurydico's mysterious death will we see that Orphea is actually the host through which the vector of digital capital infects her and her lover. To this end, we must attend to metaphorical details.

Ants are everywhere in *Orphea*. The film's opening montage shows a column of ants crawling along a stone walkway. Stop-motion then depicts large painted insects creeping up Orphea's legs and swarming around her head. In what looks like an allusion to Buñuel and Dali's *Un Chien Andalou*, another shot shows ants teeming around a hole in Orphea's hand (see fig. 38). Yet another animation sequence of a painted fresco of Orphea shows her with her guitar in hand, attacked from all sides by giant insects that amputate her hands and stimulate her severed fingers to grow to gigantic proportions (see fig. 39). Later, we see paintings of a male figure, presumably Eurydico, also infected by these very same creatures. Clearly the ersatz snake in Kluge and Khavn's retelling of the Orpheus myth, ants in *Orphea* are not the cause of any infestation of actual insects. Rather, they are a metaphor for what Kluge has elsewhere associated with Silicon Valley, its powerful algorithmic tools, and its artificial intelligence. On the one hand, this technology upstages fallible human cooperative labor with much faster, error-free forms of machine cooperation (see fig. 40). On the other hand, it has debilitating effects on matters at the core of *The Patriot*: human consciousness and perception, the valorization of human labor and property relations, autonomous subjectivity

Figures 39 and 40. *From left to right*: Orphea with her guitar, attacked by insects that amputate her limbs (her fingers have not yet been extended); robotic ants—"cooperative and accident-free"— from Kluge's 2019 installation "From Zed to Omega" at Berlin's Haus der Kulturen der Welt. © Kairos Film.

and organization, and the wish for cooperation and community.[111] That ants are the bearers of these grim technological associations is no coincidence, for Kluge has long marveled at how ants have served as a natural basis for countervailing political arguments for republicanism and totalitarianism.[112] In the context of *Orphea*, the inherently social ant allegorizes the hollowing-out of the human subject that in turn forecloses the possibility of actual sociability among people. To be sure, Orphea's recourse to biocosmism is hardly a panacea for this, or for the challenges posed by *apocatastasis*. In fact, her biocosmism merely compounds the damage done by the insects that presumably killed her lover Eurydico (not to mention her former self as Eurydice). After her seductive music fails her in the underworld, Orphea's biocosmism embraces the same messianic fantasies that inform the very real search for avatar immortality pursued by Silicon Valley's transhumanists and the venture capitalists who support them.[113] What presented itself as an absolute limit for Gabi, Orphea surmounts with a technophilia but to no avail, for her crude technology is no match for the swarm intelligence of ants.

Unlike the planned cooperation with other German directors that turned out to be so difficult in conjunction with *Germany in Autumn* and *The Patriot*, working together has proven especially fruitful for Kluge and Khavn. In fact, some critics have even been quick to draw attention to the directors' remarkable similarities. Although they are separated by continents, mother tongues, and cultures (not to mention generational experiences and eras of film history), Kluge and Khavn have appeared to some like kindred spirits on account of their prolific output and accomplishments in different métiers (Khavn is also a poet and musician), their affinity for chance and productive errors, and their shared regard for an open-ended film aesthetic.[114] What nevertheless is impossible to shrug off and should in fact be considered in our closing remarks are their significant differences. Although it would be reductive to pigeonhole Kluge as just a first-wave auteur, especially considering his considerable work in video and digital film, he is nevertheless far removed from the third cinema with which Khavn and the Philippine New Wave are often associated. In fact, scholarship has spared no effort at celebrating Khavn as an important Philippine alternative to the legacies of European colonialism, American imperialism, and neoliberal globalization that have shaped that country's national and cinematic histories.[115]

At first sight, Kluge and Khavn's film might well bring some to rashly conclude that *Orphea* is yet another example of "narrative imperialism" that privileges personalized drama, traffics in reactionary affects, and commandeers spectatorial labor all in the name of upholding the status quo.[116] Khavn himself has, however, turned the tables on any such criticisms by insisting tongue-in-cheek that "before Ovid and all the others the Orpheus myth was originally from the Philippines."[117] As if to say such chicken-or-egg questions are beside the point, Khavn's rebuttal gives us pause to assess instead how *Orphea* succeeds in accommodating two very different forms of cinematic labor that, in spite of their aesthetic differences, share an antipathy to centralization. If centralization entails stockpiling capital in one place while evacuating it from all others, then Kluge and Khavn reimagine with their Orphic myth, on the one hand, the ways in which Western techno-capital harvests total biopower not just in the West but in Asia as well. On the other hand, their differences (e.g., Khavn's Dionysian guerrilla aesthetic versus the Apollonian geometry of Kluge's montages) throw into relief all the many boundaries inscribed in the encounter between a European Orphea and a Philippine Eurydico that prevent the dispossessed of Mondomanila (where Orphea performs) and their dead loved ones from ever finding ways out of the non-spaces that make what Fredric Jameson calls the "world system" of capital possible.[118] In their own ways, Kluge and Khavn reserve no privileged place for the technology of cinema. It, too, is marked by the sign of the ant and implicated in capital's optics of surveillance and control (see figs. 41 and 42). Ways out of the reality principle, Kluge has argued, that are now governed by the algorithms of Silicon Valley only present themselves in the relationalities that emerge out of cooperation.[119] Where these ways out reside in Kluge and Khavn's cooperation are very likely situated within the film's acoustic register, the sad love songs that for Khavn explode outward to produce what Kluge has called the "musical public sphere."[120] Bearing witness musically to one's own suffering as well as that of others becomes in the end the grounds for community. To unpack Kluge and Khavn's happy lament would require, however, another book-length inquiry.

Acknowledging the common threads that bind *The Patriot* and *Orphea* is to recognize the historical context of *The Patriot* receding into the horizon as well as to engage the very different terrain on which capitalism operates today. Unlike *Orphea*, *The Patriot* robustly pads its narrative with ample constellations of thought-images that frame why Gabi does what she does, using the language of the essay film. Anyone who watches *Orphea* can acquire a deep appreciation of the theoretical foundations that shape Kluge's longstanding interest in *apocatastasis* and the history of labor power by also screening *The Patriot*. Conversely, what *Orphea* can provide our disquisition of *The Patriot* is an answer to the question stemming from the English translation of the original German title—does resistance have a gender?—and that respectfully sidesteps the quandary sparked by

Figures 41 and 42. *Above and below*: A portrait of the filmmaker marked by the sign of the ant at work painting ants (Khavn); a watch tower and surveillance cameras protecting Europe's borders (Kluge). © Kairos Film.

Kluge's bygone rallying cry for the "productive power of women." It will be recalled that beginning in the seventies feminists began charging Kluge with having ignored the question of sexual difference in both his films and his theory co-authored with Negt. The heroines featured in his early films, for example, proved for feminist critics to be mute vessels through which Kluge's own masculine desire for a politics of refusal spoke. Given this gendered division of cinematic labor, the productive force of fantasy that these films were supposed to activate in the spectators' minds provided neither points of identification nor any visual pleasure necessary for the autonomy and desires of female spectators to unfold.[121] What's more, the centrality of production in his and Negt's theories of the counter-public sphere and obstinacy fell woefully short for feminists, insofar as they equate feminine production with motherhood and never fully consider how femininity and sexual difference must be figured into women's emancipation.[122]

When applied to *The Patriot*, these criticisms have singled out not only Gabi's inability to formulate her own questions and to speak, but also, in the first place, the "grammatical impossibility" of being a female patriot that her position within the diegesis is supposed to occupy.[123] "A woman patriot doesn't even exist," feminist director Helke Sander once exclaimed, because "a patriot is part of the patriarchy."[124] If, however, we can agree that the root of Kluge's idea for Gabi's patriotism is located not in any hegemonic German patriarchy but rather in the experiences of the dispossessed subaltern first articulated by the exiled Jewish German poet Heine, then the expanded geographic frame in *Orphea* that Khavn's collaboration with Kluge makes possible suggests that Heine's dream of a universal patriotism that informs *The Patriot* must open up to include more than just a masculine/feminine binary. Yes, resistance in *Orphea* does have a gender, but it also has a sexuality, a race, an ethnicity, and a class affiliation that complicate and even confound the feminist criticisms of *The Patriot*. We might grasp the patriotic wish in *Orphea* as being far more global in scope—a patriotism loyal to regional particularities opposed to the algorithms fueling global capitalism's push for centralization—as a wish intent on bringing back *all* humanity's dead, even the subaltern voices of Mondomanila otherwise forgotten and ignored. This patriotic wish for *apokatastasis pantōn* cannot ignore, however, the unevenness of capital's development around the globe. (This is, incidentally, why Kluge and Negt gutted whole chapters about German history for the English translation of *History and Obstinacy*.[125]) And thus Kluge and Khavn put forth a metamorphosis of Ovid's Orpheus myth in which men and women switch gender roles in order to circumvent the myth's melancholic ending. Yet their figures' respective inscriptions into the unevenness of history around the globe suggest that shape-shifting strategies from below are themselves uneven. Even though techno-capital may see all bodies as alike, Orphea's and Eurydico's are not. The very different spaces within the world system they call home—Europe and Asia—ensure that they see the afterlife differently. For most, the afterlife will remain an eschatological mystery, while for a very few it appears like a problem that money and technology can solve. In the end, the totality that such a technophilic solution promises in *Orphea* lacks precisely what Gabi and Corporal Wieland's knee together show to be fundamental for grasping the vexed conditions for any real way out, namely the question of relationality.

CREDITS

Director:
Alexander Kluge
(Kluge refutes this designation, saying, "The
    film does not disclose a director title.")

Writer:
Alexander Kluge

Producer:
Alexander Kluge

Production Companies:
Kairos Film
Zweites Deutsches Fernsehen (ZDF)

Production Management:
Daniel Zuta
Alexander von Eschwege
Wilhelm von Braunmühl
Dr. Beate Klöckner
Karin Niebergall
Karin Petraschke

Cast:
Hannelore Hoger: Gabi Teichert, history
    teacher
Dieter Mainka: state security officer by day,
    voyeur by night
Alfred Edel: District Attorney Mr. Mürke
Alexander von Eschwege: Fred Tacke,
    officer in 1939
Beate Holle: Fred Tacke's wife Hildegard,
    née Gartmann
Kurt Jürgens: Mr. von Bock, military attaché
Willi Münch: bomb disposal expert Münch
Marius Müller-Westernhagen: television
    deliveryman
Günther Keidel: Gravedigger Bischoff
Hans Heckel: a researcher of fairy tales
Wolf Hanne: Superintendent Wedel

Hanno Loewy: Theo Mürke's son
Judith Krichbaum: Gerda Baethe
Pupils, members of a bomb disposal unit,
    a team manager, delegates at a party
    convention, teachers, department head
    and manager of the department store
    Kaufhof, a university professor, the
    gravedigger's colleague, Gabi Teichert's
    roommates, the commander of a fire
    department, an archaeologist, Jenny the
    elephant, a researcher working on cold-
    ness, Gerda Baethe's children, a peace
    researcher, Corporal Wieland's knee, and
    others.

Sound:
Peter Dick
Siegfried Moraweck
Kurt Graupner
O. Karla

Voiceover:
Alexander Kluge

Sound Mix:
Willi Schwadorf

Cinematography:
Günther Hörmann
Werner Lüring
Thomas Mauch
Jörg Schmidt-Reitwein
Margarethe von Trotta filmed the scene
    "Television in the Armed Forces
    Casino."
Roland Reuff filmed the scene "Digging is
    Always on the Border of Legality."

Film Editing:
Beate Mainka-Jellinghaus

Production Crew (Lights, Staging, Camera Assistants):
Charly Scheydt
Wolfgang Mundt
Reinhard Oefele
Rolf Gmöhling
Agape Dostewitz
Petra Hiller
Michael Kötz
Plus various local assistants

Editorial Board:
Willi Segler
Hans-Dieter Müller
Dagmar Steurer
Christl Buschmann
Helke Sander
Jürgen Habermas
Oskar Negt
Karen and Bion Steinborn

Running Time:
122 min.

Color:
Eastmancolor, with black-and-white sequences

Aspect Ratio:
1.375:1

Cameras:
Arriflex 120s Blimp
Zeiss Night Vision Device Orion B II

Film Length:
3,357 m

Negative Format:
35 mm

Cinematographic Process:
Spherical

Printed Film Format:
35 mm

Production Costs:
N/A

Release Dates:
Debut at Hamburg Film Festival, September 20, 1979.
Official release: December 7, 1979 (West Germany)

Awards:
German Film Prize 1979, Silver Band for the category of features without a plot

NOTES

1   Miriam Hansen, "Alexander Kluge, Cinema and the Public Sphere: The Construction Site of Counter-History," *Discourse* 4 (Winter 1981–82): 64.

2   Anton Kaes, *From Hitler to Heimat: The Return of History as Film* (Cambridge, MA: Harvard University Press, 1989), 124, 127–29.

3   Thomas Elsaesser, "New German Cinema and History: The Case of Alexander Kluge," *The German Cinema Book*, ed. Tim Bergfelder, Erica Carter, and Deniz Göktürk (London: BFI, 2002), 189.

4   On the rise of right-wing patriotism in Germany, see, for example, Katrin Bennhold, "A Far-Right Terrorism Suspect with a Refugee Disguise: The Tale of Franco A.," *The New York Times*, December 29, 2020: 1.

5   In reality, the conditions that informed Kluge's film are identical to those that shaped his other works completed around the same time that engaged with these events head-on. As will be explained in the following pages, these include Kluge's contributions to the omnibus film *Germany in Autumn* from 1977, his extensively revised 1978 edition of his first "novel" *The Battle* (originally published in 1964), his seminal 1979 speech "The Political as Intensity of Everyday Feelings," and the expanded book to his film, entitled *Die Patriotin: Texte/Bilder 1–6* and published in December 1979.

6   Although labor has not been entirely absent from the critical reception of Kluge's film—see, in particular, Caryl Flinn, *The New German Cinema: Music, History, and the Matter of Style* (Berkeley: University of California Press, 2004), 116–22—none has wrestled extensively with the dialogical relationship between it and Kluge and Negt's *History and Obstinacy*.

7   Alexander Kluge and Oskar Negt, *History and Obstinacy*, ed. Devin Fore, trans. Richard Langston et al. (New York: Zone Books, 2014), 73. For an overview of *History and Obstinacy*, see Fore's introduction, 15–67.

8   Kaes, *From Hitler to Heimat*, 111, 125.

9   Kluge and Negt, *History and Obstinacy*, 165, 181.

10 Theodor W. Adorno, *Negative Dialectics,* trans. E. B. Ashton (New York: Continuum, 1995), 11.

11 Uta Berg-Ganschow, Claudia Lenssen, and Sigrid Vagt, "Kein Dunkel hat seinesgleichen: Zu Alexander Kluges Film *Die Patriotin*," *Frauen und Film* 23 (1980): 7.

12 Angelika Wittlich, dir., *Alle Gefühle glauben an einen glücklichen Ausgang: Über Alexander Kluge*, on Alexander Kluge, *Seen sind für Fische Inseln: Fernseharbeiten 1987–2008* (Frankfurt am Main: Zweitausendeins, 2009), disc 14, track 3. Unless otherwise noted, this and all subsequent translations are those of the author.

13 Alexander Kluge, "Roswitha's Programme," trans. Stephen Elford, in *Alexander Kluge and the Occasional Work of a Female Slave*, ed. Jan Dawson (New York: Zoetrope, 1977), 47.

14 For West German feminism's initial attack, see Marlies Kallweit, Helke Sander, and Mädi Kemper, "Zu *Gelegenheitsarbeit einer Sklavin*," *Frauen und Film* 11 (1974): 12–25.

15 See Claudia Lenssen's contribution in Berg-Ganschow, Lenssen, and Vagt, "Kein Dunkel hat seinesgleichen," 9. The first American volley, which dates back to the early 1980s, is B. Ruby Rich, "She Says, He Says: The Power of the Narrator in Modernist Film Politics (1982–83)," in *Chick Flicks: Theories and Memories of the Feminist Film Movement* (Durham, NC: Duke University Press, 1998), 238–52.

16 Heide Schlüpmann, "Femininity as Productive Force: Kluge and Critical Theory," trans. Jamie Owen Daniel, *New German Critique* 49 (Winter 1990): 69–78.

17 One of the earliest printed English-language reviews of *Die Patriotin*, published in *Variety* in 1979, uses the translation *The Patriot*; see "Die Patriotin (The Patriot)" [October 31, 1979], in *Variety Film Reviews 1978–1980* (New York and London: Garland Publishing Inc., 1983), n.p. The first and most influential scholarly analysis of the film by Anton Kaes also settled on *The Patriot* as the English translation of the title. See Kaes, *From Hitler to Heimat*, 107–35. The title *The Female Patriot* emerged in English-language publications beginning around 1986 as the more accurate translation, but has remained arguably only an alternative title. The first major English-language scholarly publication to use this title, an article that incidentally pushes back against preceding feminist criticisms, is Michelle Langford, "Film Figures: Rainer Werner Fassbinder's *The Marriage of Maria Braun* and Alexander Kluge's *The Female Patriot*," in *Kiss Me Deadly: Feminism and Cinema for the Moment*, ed. Laleen Jayamanne (Sydney: Power Publications, 1995), 147–79.

18 For an excellent parsing of the strategic gendered contradictions of Kluge's German title, see Langford, "Film Figures," 174.

19 For a detailed list of the film's sequences, individual shots, and their respective timecodes, see Andreas Sombroek, "Einstellungsprotokoll *Die Patriotin*," in *Eine Poetik des Dazwischen: Zur Intermedialität und Intertextualität bei Alexander Kluge* (Bielefeld: transcript Verlag, 2005), 297–317. On Kluge and the essay, see Richard Langston, "The Guardian of Difference: The Essayist Alexander Kluge," in *Difference and Orientation: An Alexander Kluge Reader*, ed. Richard Langston (Ithaca, NY: Cornell University Press, 2019), 3–22.

20 Hans Richter, "The Film Essay: A New Type of Documentary Film," trans. Maria P. Alter, in *Essays on the Essay Film*, ed. Nora M. Alter and Timothy Corrigan (New York: Columbia University Press, 2017), 91.

21 The excerpts from Negt and Kluge's *Geschichte und Eigensinn*—the German original of *History and Obstinacy*— included in the book to Kluge's film are as follows: Alexander Kluge, *Die Patriotin: Texte/Bilder 1–6* (Frankfurt am Main: Zweitausendeins 1979), **26–37**, 325–29, 329–30, 332–40, **344–65**, **366–88**, 390–413, 438–43, **474–77**. These correspond closely to the following spans, respectively: Oskar Negt and Alexander Kluge,

Geschichte und Eigensinn, in *Der unterschätzte Mensch: Gemeinsame Philosophie in zwei Bänden*, vol. 2 (Frankfurt am Main: Zweitausendeins, 2001), **361–69**, 50–53, 25–26, 790–96, **375–85, 726–40**, 710–24, 20–24, **370–74**. Of the nine excerpts taken from the German original, only the following six are included in Kluge and Negt, *History and Obstinacy*, 104–6, 96, 250–55, 256–67, 88–91, 94–95. The spans from *Die Patriotin* and *Geschichte und Eigensinn* emphasized above correspond to chapters on German identity and history intentionally left out of the English translation. For an explanation of what was excised and why, see Richard Langston, "Notes on the Translation," in *History and Obstinacy*, 69–72; and Richard Langston, *Dark Matter: A Guide to Oskar Negt and Alexander Kluge* (London: Verso, 2020), 113–15.

22 Stefanie Carp, *Kriegsgeschichten: Zum Werk Alexander Kluges* (Munich: Wilhelm Fink Verlag, 1987), 43.

23 Alexander Kluge, "Nummern-Dramaturgie," in *Bestandsaufnahme: Utopie Film*, ed. Alexander Kluge (Frankfurt am Main: Zweitausendeins, 1983), 105–7. See also Langston, *Dark Matter*, 281–85.

24 This and all subsequent quotations are transcribed directly from the film and translated by the author. Kluge's transcription—Kluge, *Die Patriotin*, 39–179—is cited only when referring to directorial cues not obvious from screening the film. In spite of its occasional errors and omissions, Kluge's transcript is highly recommended for anyone wishing to decipher the film at the granular level.

25 On the music in *The Patriot*, especially this sequence, see Roger Hillman, "Alexander Kluge's Songs without Words," in *Unsettling Scores: German Film, Music, and Ideology* (Bloomington: Indiana University Press, 2005), 98–100.

26 Kluge's most explicit engagement with the Holocaust is: Alexander Kluge, *Anyone Who Utters a Consoling Word Is a Traitor: 48 Stories for Fritz Bauer*, trans. Alta L. Price (Seagull Books, London, 2020). His earliest Shoah story dates back to the 1962 storybook *Attendance List for a Funeral*, his first, later re-released as *Case Studies*.

27 For English-language excerpts from the book *Die Patriotin* (pages 40–42, 280–81, 294–96, 300–301) that include, in part, Kluge's programmatic notes to the film, see Alexander Kluge, "On Film and the Public Sphere," trans. Thomas Y. Levin and Miriam B. Hansen, in *Alexander Kluge: Raw Materials for the Imagination*, ed. Tara Forrest (Amsterdam: Amsterdam University Press, 2012), 33.

28 Kluge, *Die Patriotin*, 41.

29 Kluge, "On Film and the Public Sphere," 37.

30 Alexander Kluge, "The Sharpest Ideology: That Reality Appeals to its Realistic Character," trans. David Roberts, in *Alexander Kluge: Raw Materials for the Imagination*, 191. This originally appeared in the aforementioned essay collection *Gelegenheitsarbeit einer Sklavin* (1974), in which Kluge articulates his film aesthetic and his notion of the "productive power of women."

31 Ibid.

32 Alexander Kluge, *The Air Raid on Halberstadt on 8 April 1945*, trans. Martin Chalmers (London: Seagull Books, 2014), 26–32, 33–48. See also Kluge and Negt, *History and Obstinacy*, 263–65, 307–9.

33 Negt and Kluge, *Geschichte und Eigensinn*, 789. On their concepts of below and above, see Leslie Adelson, *Cosmic Miniatures and the Future Sense: Alexander Kluge's 21st-Century Literary Experiments in German Culture and Narrative Form* (Berlin: De Gruyter, 2017), 44–46, especially 45n24.

34 Kluge, "The Sharpest Ideology," 192.

35 Kluge, *Die Patriotin*, 7, 168.

36 Hans Richter, "The Badly Trained Sensibility," trans. Mike Weaver, in *The Avant-Garde Film: A Reader of Theory and Criticism*, ed. P. Adams Sitney (New York: New York University Press, 1978), 22–23.

37 Negt and Kluge, *Geschichte und Eigensinn*, 597; Alexander Kluge, "The Political as Intensity of Everyday Feelings," trans. Andrew Bowie, in *Alexander Kluge: Raw Materials for the Imagination*, 285. On immediate and remote senses in *The Patriot*, see also Christian Schulte, "Konstruktionen des Zusammenhangs: Motiv, Zeugenschaft und Wiedererkennung bei Alexander Kluge," in *Die Schrift an der Wand: Alexander Kluge; Rohstoffe und Materialien*, ed. Christian Schulte (Osnabrück: Universitätsverlag Rasch, 2000), 57.

38 Another equally suggestive allusion to Heine in *Germany in Autumn* is Wolf Biermann's poem "Was wird bloß aus unsern Träumen?" (What Will Become of Our Dreams) that echoes in part Biermann's 1972 remake of Heine's poem, also entitled "Deutschland: Ein Wintermärchen," which was republished on the eve of the events associated with the German Autumn.

39 Heinrich Heine, *Germany: A Winter's Tale*, trans. Edgar Alfred Bowring (New York: Mondial, 2007), iv.

40 Heine, *Germany: A Winter's Tale*, v. Translation slightly modified.

41 Kluge, *Die Patriotin*, 342.

42 Heine, *Germany: A Winter's Tale*, 101; "The 'Patriot,'" Kluge explained in an interview, "is a wish." See Hartmut Bitomsky, Harun Farocki, and Klaus Henrichs, "Gespräch mit Alexander Kluge: Über *Die Patriotin*, Geschichte und Filmarbeit," *Filmkritik* 23, no.11 (November 1979): 512.

43 Kluge, *Die Patriotin*, 342.

44 Kluge, "The Political as Intensity of Everyday Feelings," 288.

45 Gerhard Bechtold, "Die Sinne entspannen: Zur Multidimensionalität in Alexander Kluges Texten," in *Alexander Kluge*, ed. Thomas Böhm-Christl (Frankfurt am Main: Suhrkamp, 1983), 222–23. Cf. Kaes, *From Hitler to Heimat*, 122.

46 Kluge, *Die Patriotin*, 122.

47 For a more historical explanation of the attractive ambivalences Sibelius reception in

German offers Kluge's film, see Hillman, "Alexander Kluge's Songs without Words," 103–5.

48 Jacob W. Grimm and Wilhelm K. Grimm, "The Stubborn Child," in *Complete Fairy Tales of the Brothers Grimm*, ed. and trans. Jack Zipes (Westminster: Bantam Books, 1992), 422. The title is altered here in accordance with its usage in: Kluge and Negt, *History and Obstinacy*, 291. See also Kluge, *Die Patriotin*, 37.

49 Karl Marx, *Capital: A Critique of Political Economy*, vol. 1, trans. Ben Fowkes (London: Penguin Classics, 1990), 875.

50 Kluge and Negt, *History and Obstinacy*, 511n104.

51 Kluge and Negt, *History and Obstinacy*, 279. For Kluge and Negt's lengthy excursus on the distinction between landlocked German fairy tales and ancient epics organized around seafaring Mediterranean adventures, see their twelfth commentary in *History and Obstinacy*, 268–95.

52 Kluge and Negt, *History and Obstinacy*, 292.

53 Bitomsky, Farocki, and Henrichs, "Gespräch mit Alexander Kluge," 507.

54 Karl Marx, *The German Ideology*, in Karl Marx, *Selected Writings*, ed. David McLellan, 2nd ed. (Oxford: Oxford University Press, 2000), 188. See also Kluge and Negt, *History and Obstinacy*, 230–33.

55 Kluge and Negt, *History and Obstinacy*, 232, 280, 281.

56 Kluge and Negt, *History and Obstinacy*, 181. See also Bitomsky, Farocki, and Henrichs, "Gespräch mit Alexander Kluge," 513: "KLUGE: This simple line of thought [namely changing the raw materials according to which history is written, RL] contains the wish for community that simultaneously has something to do with [Gabi's] labor."

57 Bitomsky, Farocki, and Henrichs, "Gespräch mit Alexander Kluge," 507.

58 For a reading of anti-scopophilic regimes in *The Patriot*, see Hansen, "Alexander Kluge, Cinema and the Public Sphere," 68–70.

59 Kluge and Negt, *History and Obstinacy*, 283.

60 On Kluge's anthropological theory, see Langston, *Dark Matter*, 120–25.

61 Cf. Peter C. Lutze, *Alexander Kluge: The Last Modernist* (Detroit, MI: Wayne State University Press, 1998), 92. See also Kluge, *Die Patriotin* 141.

62 Kluge and Negt, *History and Obstinacy*, 102.

63 Alexander Kluge, "Film: A Utopia," trans. Samantha Lankford, in *Difference and Orientation*, ed. Langston, 166–67.

64 Walter Benjamin, "On the Concept of History," trans. Harry Zohn, in *Selected Writings*, ed. Howard Eiland and Michael W. Jennings, vol. 4: *1938–1940* (Cambridge, MA: The Belknap Press, 2003), 392.

65 For a succinct overview of Benjamin's thought-image, see Max Pensky, "Method and

Time: Benjamin's Dialectical Images," in *The Cambridge Companion to Walter Benjamin*, ed. David S. Ferris (Cambridge: Cambridge University Press, 2004), 179–80. On Kluge's employment of the dialectical image, see Hansen, "Alexander Kluge, Cinema and the Public Sphere," 63.

66 Kluge, "Film: A Utopia," 180. For a discussion of Kluge's destruction of images, see Philipp Ekardt, *Toward Fewer Images: The Work of Alexander Kluge* (Cambridge, MA: The MIT Press, 2018), 40–48.

67 Karl Marx, *Economic and Philosophic Manuscripts of 1844*, in Karl Marx and Frederick Engels, *Collected Works*, vol. 3: *March 1843–August 1844* (London: Lawrence and Wishart, 1975), especially 279–306. Here 279. On the theft of wood, see Karl Marx, "Proceedings of the Sixth Rhein Province Assembly: Third Article Debates on the Law on Theft of Wood," in Karl Marx and Frederick Engels, *Collected Works*, vol. 1: *August 1835–March 1843* (London: Lawrence and Wishart, 2010), 221–63.

68 Cf. Bernd Brunner, *Inventing the Christmas Tree*, trans. Benjamin A. Smith (New Haven, CT: Yale University Press, 2012), 9. See also Kristin Kopp, *Germany's Wild East: Constructing Poland as Colonial Space* (Ann Arbor: The University of Michigan Press, 2012), 57–95.

69 On the imprecision regarding when capital first started hijacking German history, Kluge replied: "Marx would certainly start 2,000 years ago. But it's all the same which dates I choose. Numbers are only suitable for capturing the fantasy." See Bitomsky, Farocki, and Henrichs, "Gespräch mit Alexander Kluge," 507.

70 For a fuller discussion of natural history, see Theodor W. Adorno, "The Idea of Natural-History," trans. Robert Hullot-Kentor, in *Things Beyond Resemblance: Collected Essays on Theodor W. Adorno*, ed. Robert Hullot-Kentor (New York: Columbia University Press, 2006), 253.

71 Ibid., 264, 262.

72 Oskar Negt and Alexander Kluge, *Public Sphere and Experience: Toward an Analysis of the Bourgeois and Proletarian Public Sphere*, trans. Peter Labanyi, Jamie Daniel, and Assenka Oksiloff (Minneapolis: University of Minnesota Press, 1993), 33.

73 Theodor W. Adorno, "Education after Auschwitz," in *Critical Models: Interventions and Catchwords*, trans. Henry Pickford (New York: Columbia University Press, 1998), 201. See also Nora M. Alter, Lutz Koepnick, and Richard Langston, "Landscapes of Ice, Snow and Wind: Alexander Kluge's Aesthetics of Coldness," *Grey Room* 53 (Fall 2013): 60–87.

74 Kluge, *Die Patriotin*, 156.

75 Kluge, *Die Patriotin*, 160. Cf. Bitomsky, Farocki, and Henrichs, "Gespräch mit Alexander Kluge," 506.

76 For a very different reading of this sequence that overlooks Schiller's fifth stanza, see Flinn, *The New German Cinema*, 12–17, 125–26, 136–37.

77 This is from the standard English translation in: Ludwig van Beethoven, *9 Symphonien*, Berliner Philharmoniker, Herbert von Karajan, Deutsche Grammaphon, CD 429036–2, 1978, liner notes.

78 Theodor W. Adorno, *Beethoven: The Philosophy of Music*, ed. Rolf Tiedemann, trans. Edmund Jephcott (Cambridge: Polity, 2002), 33.

79 Ibid. Adorno's choice of antiquated language here—"alten Jungfern" in the German original is rendered as "old maids" in the translation—is arguably not only patronizing, but its sexism also undermines his case against Schiller. See Theodor W. Adorno, *Beethoven: Philosophie der Musik, Fragmente und Texte*, ed. Rolf Tiedemann (Frankfurt am Main: Suhrkamp, 1993), 60.

80 Ursula Marx, Gudrun Schwarz, Michael Schwarz, and Erdmut Wizisla, eds., *Walter Benjamin's Archive: Images, Texts, Signs*, trans. Esther Leslie (New York: Verso, 2007), 45.

81 In this respect, it is arguable that Gabi's search resonates with the Frankfurt School's own "preference for the particular." "Critical Theory imagines the universal as an elementary undercurrent *beneath* the particular (similar to the labor of partisans) or *immanently* in the midst of the particular." Kluge and Negt, *History and Obstinacy*, 198. See also note 8.

82 Benjamin, "On the Concept of History," 390; Walter Benjamin, *The Arcades Project*, ed. Rolf Tiedemann, trans. Howard Eiland and Kevin McLaughlin (Cambridge, MA: The Belknap Press, 1999), 698 [a1,1].

83 Michael Löwy, *Fire Alarm: Reading Walter Benjamin's "On the Concept of History,"* trans. Chris Turner (New York: Verso, 2005), 36.

84 On the Marxist history of cooperation between agrarian and urban laborers, see Kluge, *Die Patriotin*, 382.

85 Kluge and Negt, *History and Obstinacy*, 102.

86 Negt and Kluge, *Public Sphere and Experience*, 34; see also Kluge, "On Film and the Public Sphere," 37–38.

87 Negt and Kluge have repeatedly equated the standpoint of emancipation under capitalist rule as something "non-cohesive" (*nicht-zusammenhängendes*). This non-cohesiveness is the answer to the question of relationality. See Negt and Kluge, *Public Sphere and Experience*, 296; Kluge and Negt, *History and Obstinacy*, 220.

88 Whereas Kaes sees the film's ending on New Year's Eve as a hopeful nod to Gabi's anticipation of "new stories, new experiences, and new memories," others like Flinn regard the concluding sequence uncritically positive. See Kaes, *From Hitler to Heimat*, 135; and Flinn, *The New German Cinema*, 136–37.

89 Bitomsky, Farocki, and Henrichs, "Gespräch mit Alexander Kluge," 513.

90 Kluge, *Die Patriotin*, 7.

91 Ibid.

80

92 On the "contradictions and inconsistencies" in *Germany in Autumn* that hampered the plans for other directors to collaborate on *The Patriot*, see Miriam Hansen, "Cooperative Auteur Cinema and Oppositional Public Sphere: Alexander Kluge's Contribution to *Germany in Autumn*," *New German Critique* 24/25 (Autumn 1981–Winter 1982): 36–56.

93 Kluge, *Die Patriotin*, 284, 281, 23.

94 Kluge, *Die Patriotin*, 42. Translation modified as compared to Kluge, "On Film and the Public Sphere," 34.

95 One of Kluge's earliest formulations of the film in the spectator's head can be found in Alexander Kluge, "Bits of Conversation," trans. Emma Woelk, in *Difference and Orientation*, ed. Langston, 142–54.

96 Kluge, "On Film and the Public Sphere," 38, 37.

97 Kluge, *Die Patriotin*, 381.

98 Kluge and Negt, *History and Obstincy*, 292–95.

99 Odysseus plays, of course, a central role as the embodiment of bourgeois subjectivity in Max Horkheimer and Adorno's *Dialectic of Enlightenment*, and volume one of Peter Weiss's *The Aesthetics of Resistance* prominently features Heracles as the mascot of the proletariat.

100 Alexander Kluge in discussion with the author, June 2018.

101 Marx, *Capital*, vol. 1, 777.

102 Alexander Kluge, "Reading and Writing: How Can I Live? What Can I Know? What Does the Future Hold?" in *The New Alphabet: Opening Days*, ed. Bernd Scherer and Olga von Schubert (Berlin: HKW, 2019), 38.

103 Kolja Reichert, "'Künstler sind Pilotfischchen': Alexander Kluge im Interview," *Frankfurter Allgemeine Zeitung*, October 19, 2017, http://www.faz.net/-gsa-92vbx.

104 Kluge, "Reading and Writing," 38.

105 Kluge and Negt, *History and Obstinacy*, 141.

106 Kluge, *Die Patriotin*, 169.

107 Kluge and Khavn's trilogy began with *Happy Lamento* (2018), continues with *Orphea* (2020), and concludes with *Cold Death Interrupts Love* (*Die Liebe stört der kalte Tod*), which has not yet been released.

108 Alexander Kluge and Richard Langston, "'Happy Is the Last Man Standing!' From Independent Cinema to Auteur Television and Back Again," *Alexander Kluge-Jahrbuch* 6 (2019): 239.

109 Cf. Boris Groys, "Introduction: Russian Cosmism and the Technology of Immortality," *Russian Cosmism*, ed. Boris Groys (New York: e-flux, 2018), 7.

110 Kluge, "The Political as Intensity of Everyday Feelings," 286.

111 Arguably, Kluge's most explicit reference to ants and artificial intelligence is found in his 2019 film "Mondrian-Maschine Nr. 1," which begins with excerpts from *The Patriot* and includes sequences of insect robots in operation (see fig. 40). For a transcript, see Alexander Kluge, "Von Zett bis Omega: 'Begehbares Theater—Ein Babylon dessen Turm nicht zerfällt, in Berlin,'" *Alexander Kluge-Jahrbuch* 6 (2019): 155–96. The film from which figure 40 is taken can be viewed at https://www.dctp.tv/filme/mondrian-maschine-nr-1-ulm.

112 See, for example, Alexander Kluge, "Ameisen ('das politische Tier'): Prof. Dr. Niels Werber: Das Narrativ von den sozialen Insekten," *News & Stories*, SAT.1, August 17, 2014, https://www.dctp.tv/filme/ ameisen_newsstories_17082014. See also Kluge and Negt, *History and Obstinacy*, 402.

113 For an overview of the principal features of Silicon Valley's transhumanism and the search for avatar immortality, see Jenny Huberman, "From Ancestors to Avatars: Transfiguring the Afterlife," *The Routledge Handbook of Death and Afterlife*, ed. Candi K. Cann (New York: Routledge, 2018), 280–85.

114 See, for example, Sofie Cato Maas, "Orphea: Eye-popping and nose-exploding?" *Frameland: A Monthly Magazine*, May 2020, https://frame.land/orphea-eye-popping-and-nose-exploding.

115 See, for example, William Brown, "Digital Darkness in the Philippines," in *Non-Cinema: Global Digital Filmmaking and the Multitude* (New York: Bloomsbury Academic, 2018), 87–111.

116 Jonathan Beller, "Iterations of the Impossible: Questions of a Digital Revolution in the Philippines," *Postcolonial Studies* 11, no. 4 (2008): 435, 436, 437.

117 Knut Elsterman, "Berlinale Talk 2020 mit Alexander Kluge, Khavn de la Cruz und Lilith Stangenberg," Der Berlinale Talk, Radio Eins, Rundfunk Berlin Brandenburg, Feb. 25, 2020, accessed June 14, 2020, https://www.youtube.com/watch?v=-8fi-Bgd9WY.

118 Fredric Jameson, *The Geopolitical Aesthetic: Cinema and Space in the World System* (Bloomington: Indiana University Press, 1992). *Mondomanila* is also the title of Khavn's 2012 film based on Norman Wilwayco's 2002 novel of the same name.

119 Kluge, "The Political as Intensity of Everyday Feelings," 286.

120 Khavn de la Cruz, Interview with Pamela Cohn, *Bomb Magazine*, September 29, 2010, https://bombmagazine.org/articles/khavn-de-la-cruz; see also Alexander Kluge, "The Equivalent of an Oasis: An Essay for the Digital Generation," trans. Richard Langston, *Alexander Kluge-Jahrbuch* 6 (2019): 201; and Reichert's interview (cited above), in which Kluge states: "We would have to combine everything that the arts can achieve including music in order to create counter-algorithms against Silicon Valley."

121 Heide Schlüpmann, "'What Is Different Is Good': Women and Femininity in the Films of Alexander Kluge," trans. Jamie Owen Daniel, *October* 46 (Autumn 1988): 132, 138, 150.

122 Schlüpmann, "Femininity as Productive Force," 72.

123 Helke Sander, "'You Can't Always Get What You Want': The Films of Alexander Kluge," trans. Regina Cornwell, *New German Critique* 49 (Winter 1990): 65.

124 Ibid.

125 On the unevenness of capitalism's development, see Kluge and Negt, *History and Obstinacy*, 218–22.

Printed in the United States
by Baker & Taylor Publisher Services